MADE

100 of the WORLD'S BEST CHEFS, cooks & FOOD ARTISANS

WITH

& the food they make for the PEOPLE THEY LOVE

LOVE

MADE

100 of the WORLD'S BEST CHEFS, cooks & FOOD ARTISANS

WITH

& the food they make for the PEOPLE THEY LOVE

LOVE

PQ Blackwell

Among Nelson Mandela's personal papers in the Nelson Mandela Foundation's archive is a wonderful letter about food in which Madiba writes to his two daughters on their developing culinary skills. Reading that letter reiterates to me how much he appreciated good food and recognised that preparing and sharing food was one of the simplest ways to show love for others.

Unfortunately, what should be a simple, achievable act for anyone – providing food for loved ones – is a struggle for far too many. Today, one in four South Africans suffers from hunger, and in some parts of the country one in six children suffers from severe malnutrition. Food insecurity is fuelled by chronic levels of inequality and coupled with drought and high levels of unemployment. In order to reverse these alarming statistics, food security is now a major focus of Mandela Day, a global movement to change the world for the better, led by the Nelson Mandela Foundation.

I am delighted, therefore, that the publication of *Made With Love* will directly support the Foundation's food-security work. Drawn from the bestselling 'Great' cookbook series, which was launched in 2014 with *The Great New Zealand Cookbook*, followed by *The Great Australian Cookbook* in 2015, *The Great South African Cookbook* in 2016 and the latest addition to the series, *The Really Quite Good British Cookbook*, it is not only a joyous culinary celebration of cuisine from around the world but also proceeds from sales of the book will be used to develop and support community food and agricultural projects.

I would like to extend a heartfelt thanks to each and every one of the contributors from around the world for agreeing to be part of this book. By inviting us to your homes, restaurants, farms and communities and sharing the food you cook for the people you love, you have helped improve the lives of those who are in need of food and who need to be freed from poverty. Thank you also to South African artist Conrad Botes, whose striking image of Nelson Mandela appears opposite.

On the occasion of his 90th birthday, Mandela said: "The world remains beset by so much suffering, poverty and deprivation. It is in your hands to make of our world a better one for all, especially the poor, vulnerable and marginalised." For me, this book is about hope for what can be achieved both now and in the future, and, ultimately, about sharing and changing lives with food.

Sello Hatang
Chief Executive
Nelson Mandela Foundation

CONTENTS

Diep River,
Western Cape

CASS ABRAHAMS
AUTHOR & CAPE MALAY CHEF

I realised early on in my career that when you see a plate of food in front of you, you can tell a lot about the history, the geography and the economics of its originating country. Food builds bridges over culture and class systems. We were so separated under apartheid in South Africa, and food broke down those walls that divided us.

THREE-DHAL CURRY

Recipe by *CASS ABRAHAMS*, author & Cape Malay chef, Western Cape, South Africa

SERVINGS: 6 | PREP TIME: 20 MINS PLUS 30 MINS SOAKING | COOK TIME: 30–45 MINS
SKILL LEVEL: 1 (EASY)

INGREDIENTS

125 ml oil dhal
  (also known as toor
  dhal or yellow lentils)
125 ml moong dhal
125 ml channa dhal
1 large onion, thinly sliced
60 ml oil
2 sticks cassia
  (I use Robertsons)
2 cardamom pods
1 sprig curry leaves
2 medium-sized tomatoes,
  skinned and chopped
½ tsp chilli flakes
  (I use Robertsons)
10 tsp crushed garlic
5 tsp crushed ginger
2 tsp garam masala
5 tsp ground cumin
  (I use Robertsons)
5 tsp ground coriander
  (I use Robertsons)
5 tsp ground turmeric
  (I use Robertsons)
about 3 cups water
salt to taste
250 g chopped
  coriander leaves

DF, GF, V

METHOD

Soak all the dhals in a bowl of water for 30 minutes. Place onion, oil, cassia, cardamom and curry leaves in a large saucepan and fry until onions are soft.

Add tomatoes, chilli flakes, garlic, ginger and all the spices and stir well. Drain the dhals and add to the pan together with 3 cups water. Season to taste. Bring to the boil and simmer until dhal is soft and mushy.

Sprinkle with coriander leaves and serve with rice or puri (an unleavened, deep-fried, flaky Indian bread).

TOM AIKENS
TOM'S KITCHEN

My mother was definitely the first inspiration on my path to becoming a chef. We lived in Norfolk with a big garden and she would drag us out of the house and get us gardening — weeding, picking, sowing and planting. We would then take the fruit and vegetables and make them into anything from chutneys to jams.

Tom

*Chelsea,
London*

ROASTED PLUMS WITH CARDAMOM CARAMEL

Recipe by *TOM AIKENS*, Tom's Kitchen, London, England

SERVINGS: 4 | **PREP TIME: 10 MINS** | **COOK TIME: 15 MINS** | **SKILL LEVEL: 1 (EASY)**

There is a lovely balance of sweet and spicy flavours in this dish, which is also very quick to make.

INGREDIENTS

For the spiced crème fraîche
300 g crème fraîche
80 g caster sugar
1 tsp ground cinnamon
seeds from a split vanilla pod

2 tbsp muscovado sugar
a large pinch of mixed spice
a small pinch of ground cloves
a large pinch of ground ginger
a pinch of five-spice powder
2 cardamom pods, finely crushed
finely grated zest of 2 oranges
3 tbsp unsalted butter, softened
1 tbsp brioche crumbs
12 ripe plums, cut in half and
  stones removed

V

METHOD

Put the crème fraîche in a bowl with the sugar, cinnamon and vanilla seeds and beat with a wooden spoon for 3–4 minutes.

Pre-heat the oven to 200°C. Mix the muscovado sugar, spices, orange zest, butter and brioche crumbs in a bowl. Put the plums in a baking tin and add a little of the crumb mixture on each half. Bake in the pre-heated oven for 15 minutes, or place under a hot grill until the plums start to caramelise. Serve hot or cold with spiced crème fraîche.

STEPHANIE ALEXANDER AO
CHEF, RESTAURATEUR & FOOD WRITER

One of the ways to enthuse people who may feel anxious about cooking is to suggest cooking something which is really only about three or four steps. And when it comes out of the oven, it really is so good, that they're going to do it again and again and again.

Stephanie

Abbotsford, Victoria

SIMPLEST BEEF STEW

Recipe by *STEPHANIE ALEXANDER* AO, chef, restaurateur & food writer, Victoria, Australia

SERVINGS: 4–6 | **PREP TIME: 10 MINS** | **COOK TIME: 2 HOURS (APPROX.)** | **SKILL LEVEL: 1 (EASY)**

INGREDIENTS

1½ kg chuck (or blade) steak, cut into large cubes

60 g plain flour

2 tsp best-quality paprika

1 x 400 g can peeled tomatoes in juice

1 glass (250–300 ml) white (or red) wine

1 cup beef stock (or water)

2 onions, diced

2 cloves garlic, sliced

1 stick celery, finely sliced

3 carrots, peeled and cut into chunks

1 fresh (or dried) bay leaf

DF

METHOD

Pre-heat oven to 180°C.

Roll beef in flour mixed with paprika (easiest to do this in a plastic bag). Put into a lidded casserole dish that will hold the ingredients comfortably with not too much extra space.

Whizz tomatoes and their juice in a food processor, or crush roughly with a wooden spoon, and add to meat. Add remaining ingredients to casserole and stir. The meat should be almost covered by liquid.

Press a piece of baking paper over contents and cover with lid. Cook in oven, undisturbed, for 2 hours. Taste for seasoning, and add salt and freshly ground black pepper to taste. Check whether meat is tender, and cook longer if necessary – give it another 20 minutes and then check again.

Offer stew with a bowl of yoghurt and maybe a small bowl of sliced pickled dill cucumbers.

BAKEWELL PUDDING

Recipe by *GERARD BAKER*, chef, food historian & radio presenter, East Riding, England

SERVINGS: 6 | **PREP TIME: 20 MINS PLUS RESTING** | **COOK TIME: 1½ HOUR** | **SKILL LEVEL: 2 (MODERATE)**

Mrs Beeton used puff pastry for her Bakewell pudding, but a well-baked shortcrust tart case is a better match, giving a crisp contrast to the rich, silky filling. Use homemade raspberry jam if you have it, or choose a sharp conserve to contrast with the sweet filling.

INGREDIENTS

For the pastry

250 g plain flour

pinch of salt

125 g cold unsalted butter, cubed or grated

½ tsp lemon juice

100 ml iced water

For the filling

115 g butter

160 g caster sugar

30 g ground almonds

5 egg yolks

1 egg white

80g sharp, best-quality raspberry jam

Special equipment

a deep 22 cm metal pie dish

some baking beans

V

METHOD

First make the pastry. If you have a food processor, sift the flour and salt into the bowl and mix. Add the cubed butter and pulse until the mixture resembles fine breadcrumbs. Pour the mixture into a bowl.

If you are working by hand, sift the flour and salt into a bowl and add the cubed or grated butter. Rub the butter and flour between your fingertips until it resembles fine breadcrumbs, working quickly to keep the mixture as cool as possible. If it starts to feel sticky, chill the mixture for 30 minutes before moving on to the next step.

Add the lemon juice to the water and pour two-thirds of this into the flour mixture. Blend well with a fork, stirring quickly but gently. Using your fingertips, bring the dough together. Add more lemon-water as necessary (you may need to use all of it), until everything is evenly mixed and there are no dry lumps of flour. Bring the mixture together into a smooth, supple lump. Carefully form the pastry into a flattened ball, wrap in clingfilm and chill for 20 minutes.

Then, roll the pastry out on a floured surface to a 27 cm round. Place it in the pie dish, leaving the extra pastry hanging over the edge. Line the pastry with a large piece of non-stick baking paper and then fill with baking beans. Leave to rest in a cool place for 10 minutes.

Pre-heat the oven to 200°C.

Place the pastry case on a baking tray and bake for 35 minutes until firm and golden-brown. Remove the beans and paper and return the case to the oven for 5 minutes to bake further and dry slightly. Remove from the oven and set aside. Reduce the oven to 160°C.

Make the filling by melting the butter in a medium saucepan over a low heat. Remove from the heat, and add the sugar, ground almonds and egg yolks and white, beating well to combine.

Spread the jam into the pastry case and carefully pour over the filling. Bake for 15 minutes, then turn the oven down to 140°C for a further 30 minutes until the filling is just firm to the touch. Trim the pastry hanging over the rim with a sharp knife, and cool to room temperature before serving.

MAGGIE BEER AM
COOK, RESTAURATEUR & AUTHOR

I have loved quinces for 42 years, from the moment
I came to live in the valley from New South Wales
where I was a city girl. And with every farmhouse
I ever visited in the Barossa, looking for what we
wanted to buy ourselves, there was always a quince
tree. Sometimes the cottages were derelict but the
quince tree would survive. We planted our first quince
orchard nearly 30 years ago and we're still planting
quinces now – that's how much I love them.

Maggie

*Barossa Valley,
South Australia*

CHOCOLATE, QUINCE & ALMOND TART

Recipe by *MAGGIE BEER AM*, cook, restaurateur & author, South Australia, Australia

SERVINGS: 10–12 | **PREP TIME: 50 MINS** | **COOK TIME: 3¾–4 HOURS** | **SKILL LEVEL: 2 (MODERATE)**

INGREDIENTS

For the pot-roasted quinces

500 g quinces, peeled, cored and cut into large wedges

a squeeze of lemon juice

250 ml water

150 ml verjuice (plus an extra 100 ml if needed)

140 g caster sugar

For the chocolate and almond cream

90 g unsalted butter, softened

110 g caster sugar

2 free-range eggs

1 free-range egg yolk

40 g dark chocolate cocoa

60 ml vino cotto

150 g ground almond meal

To finish

1 x 300 g packet Carême dark chocolate shortcrust pastry

crème fraîche or mascarpone, to serve

V

METHOD

Pre-heat a fan-forced oven to 190°C/170°C fan.

As you peel and core the quinces, place then in a pot of water with the squeeze of lemon juice. This will help stop them oxidising.

To pot-roast the quinces, place the quinces, 250 ml of water, verjuice and caster sugar in a medium-sized heavy-based ovenproof pot. Place this over a high heat and bring to the boil, cover with a lid and place in the oven. Cook for 1 hour, then remove the lid and give the quinces a very light toss, making sure not to break up the wedges.

Place back in the oven and cook for another 1–1½ hours. Check the quinces every 15–20 minutes to make sure that the liquid has not all evaporated; if it starts to, and they look like they will catch on the bottom, add an extra 100 ml of verjuice.

Once the quinces are cooked they should be a beautiful ruby-red colour with a small amount of syrup in the base of the pot. They should not be dry or caught on the base of the pot. Remove the quinces and place on a plate or tray to cool.

Increase the oven temperature to 220°C/200°C fan.

To make the chocolate and almond cream, place the butter and caster sugar in a food processor and beat on high until light and creamy (approximately 6 minutes). With the processor still running, add the eggs and yolk (one at a time), then the cocoa and vino cotto and mix for a further minute. Add the almond meal and mix until well combined. Set aside until ready to use.

To finish, grease a flan tin (24 cm x 2½ cm) and line with the pastry. Cut off the excess pastry around the edge but allow the pastry to come above the tin by 5 mm, to allow for shrinkage during blind-baking. Place in the fridge for 15 minutes to chill.

Remove the chilled tart shell from the fridge, spike the bottom with a fork, line the top with non-stick baking paper and place blind-baking beans on top (ordinary dried beans or rice work just as well). Bake for 15 minutes, then remove the beans and paper and cook for a further 5 minutes.

Remove the tart shell and reduce the oven temperature to 195°C/175°C fan.

Place a third of the chocolate and almond cream on the base of the tart shell. Top with cooked quince wedges and dot the remaining chocolate and almond cream on top. Return the tart to the oven for 50–60 minutes; this time will depend on your oven, but you need to make sure that the chocolate and almond cream is cooked in the centre.

Remove from the oven and allow to cool. Serve with crème fraîche or mascarpone.

APRICOT & ALMOND TORTE

Recipe by *MARY BERRY CBE*, food writer & TV presenter, Buckinghamshire, England

SERVINGS: 8 | **PREP TIME: 30 MINS** | **COOK TIME: 20–25 MINS** | **SKILL LEVEL: 1 (EASY)**

Perfect for a Sunday lunch, this is a very thin, golden dessert served with crème fraîche or pouring cream. This torte is best made and served immediately, but if you have some left over it reheats well the next day. If you have an Aga, bake the torte on the grid shelf on the floor of the roasting oven for 20–25 minutes. If it's getting too brown, slide a cold sheet onto the second set of runners.

INGREDIENTS

75 g butter, softened,
  plus extra for greasing
75 g caster sugar
75 g self-raising flour
25 g ground almonds
1 tsp baking powder
1 tsp almond extract
2 eggs
2 x 400 g cans apricot
  halves in juice
3 tbsp apricot jam
50 g toasted flaked
  almonds

V

METHOD

Pre-heat the oven to 200°C/180°C fan. Grease a 28 cm fluted loose-bottomed tin with butter.

Measure the butter, sugar, flour, ground almonds, baking powder, almond extract and eggs into a bowl. Beat together until smooth. Spread out over the base of the greased tin.

Drain the apricots and dry with kitchen paper. Arrange, cut-side down, over the surface of the mixture. Bake for about 20–25 minutes, until the sponge is lightly golden-brown and well risen.

Melt the jam in a saucepan over a low heat until just melted. Brush over the sponge and apricots and scatter with the flaked almonds. Remove the torte from the tin while warm and serve cut into wedges.

CHERRY CLAFOUTIS

Recipe by *RAYMOND BLANC OBE, CLH*, Belmond Le Manoir aux Quat'Saisons, Oxford, England

SERVINGS: 4 | **PREP TIME: 30 MINS PLUS 2 HOURS MACERATING** | **COOK TIME: 30–35 MINS**
SKILL LEVEL: I (EASY)

Clafoutis is one of the great classics of French family cuisine. This dessert often features on our menus, both at Le Manoir and at Brasserie Blanc. It is very easy to prepare and I would go so far as to say it is foolproof. Other stone-fruits, such as peaches, plums and apricots, or indeed figs, work just as well.

INGREDIENTS

For the cherries

450 g best-quality cherries (such as Montmorency or Morello), stoned

50 g caster sugar, plus extra for sprinkling

2–3 tbsp kirsch, to taste (optional)

For preparing the dish

10 g unsalted butter, melted

30 g caster sugar, plus extra to finish (optional)

For the batter

2 organic/free-range medium-sized eggs

45 g caster sugar

½ tsp vanilla extract

20 g unsalted butter

20 g plain flour

50 ml whole milk

75 ml whipping cream

pinch sea salt

Special equipment

a 20 cm round ceramic or cast-iron baking dish

a cherry stoner

V

METHOD

To prepare the cherries: gently mix together the cherries, sugar and kirsch, if using, in a bowl. Leave to macerate for 2 hours (see note below).

Pre-heat the oven to 180°C.

To prepare the dish: brush the inside with the melted butter. Add the sugar and tilt the dish to coat the sides and base evenly; shake out the excess.

To make the clafoutis: in a large bowl whisk together the eggs, sugar and vanilla until creamy. Meanwhile, melt the butter in a small pan until it turns a pale hazelnut colour – this is called a beurre noisette (see note 2). Add the flour to the egg and sugar mixture and whisk until smooth, then slowly incorporate the milk, cream, salt and beurre noisette. Stir in the cherries with their juices and then pour into the prepared baking dish.

To cook the clafoutis: bake in the oven for 30–35 minutes until the clafoutis is lightly risen and a knife inserted in the middle comes out clean (see note 3). Leave to stand for about 10 minutes. Sprinkle with caster sugar, if using, and serve just warm.

NOTES

While macerating, the sugar slowly permeates the fruit and intensifies the taste.

The foaming butter will turn a hazelnut colour at 150–155°C, i.e. beurre noisette. This butter will lend a wonderful roundness and nutty flavour to the clafoutis.

The centre is always the last part to cook, so you must test it. Note that a dip in the middle suggests the clafoutis is undercooked.

Cape Town,
Western Cape

JAN BRAAI
AUTHOR & FOUNDER OF NATIONAL BRAAI DAY

African bird's-eye or piri-piri chillies are my first choice for this sauce –
they are small and very hot – but you can use any small, potent chillies.
The very best option is to grow your own.

This sauce will improve with age and keeps for several weeks in the fridge.

Jan

BRAAI FREEDOM-FIGHTER BURGER

Recipes by *JAN BRAAI*, author & founder of National Braai Day, Western Cape, South Africa

**SERVINGS: 4 | PREP TIME: 10 MINS PLUS FIRE PREPARATION | COOK TIME: 8 MINS PLUS RESTING
SKILL LEVEL: 1 (EASY)**

INGREDIENTS

2 tbsp olive oil

2 red onions, sliced or
  chopped

2 sweet red capsicum

2 cloves garlic, crushed
  or chopped

1 tsp chilli powder or
  cayenne pepper

2 tbsp paprika

2 tomatoes, chopped

2 tbsp tomato paste

½ cup beef stock

1 kg steak mince

1 tsp sea salt

1 tsp ground black pepper

4 hamburger rolls, buttered

sour cream, to serve

chopped fresh parsley,
  to serve

METHOD

Heat the oil in a pan or potjie and fry the onions and capsicum for about 4 minutes until they start to soften, then throw in the garlic. Add the chilli powder or cayenne pepper and paprika and stir to release their flavours. Add the tomatoes, tomato paste and beef stock, and stir to combine. Bring to the boil, reduce the heat to a simmer, and allow the flavours to develop and the sauce to thicken. Check the pan or potjie every now and then to stir the sauce and make sure it doesn't cook dry or burn.

Meanwhile, wet your hands with water and divide the mince into four equal-sized patties. Shape them into rounds, flattening them out quite well, as they will shrink a little during the braaiing process. Sprinkle with salt and pepper on both sides just before or during braaiing. Braai them over very hot coals for 8 minutes, turning only once.

Remove the patties from the braai and rest them for a few minutes. Meanwhile, briefly toast the insides of the buttered rolls on the braai for bonus points. Assemble the burger as follows: roll, patty, sauce, dollop of sour cream, chopped parsley. Serve immediately.

PERI-PERI SAUCE

SERVINGS: 10 (1 MEDIUM-SIZED JAR) | PREP TIME: 10 MINS | COOK TIME: 30 MINS | SKILL LEVEL: 1 (EASY)

INGREDIENTS

8 cloves garlic, finely
  chopped

½ cup oil

½ cup grape vinegar
  (red or white)

½ cup lemon juice

½ cup water

2 tbsp paprika

2 tbsp chilli powder

2 tbsp coarse salt

a few small, hot chillies
  (see tips)

GF, DF, V

METHOD

Put the garlic, oil, vinegar, lemon juice, water, paprika, chilli powder and salt in a glass jar. Close the lid tightly and shake well until the ingredients are mixed and all the salt has dissolved. Taste the sauce and start adding chopped fresh chilli to taste.

TIPS

Remember that your guests might like much less heat than you do – I often make two batches of this sauce, one with fewer chillies than the other.

Remember not to touch your eyes or any other sensitive parts of your body while making this sauce, as you will burn yourself. As soon as you are finished preparing it, wash your hands thoroughly (and then still be careful).

PLAITED SCONES

Recipe by *DEAN BRETTSCHNEIDER*, author & TV presenter, Canterbury, New Zealand

MAKES: 2 (1 SWEET, 1 SAVOURY) | PREP TIME: 25 MINS PLUS STANDING | COOK TIME: 30–35 MINS
SKILL LEVEL: 2 (MODERATE)

INGREDIENTS

For the sweet filling
100 g dates,
  pitted and chopped
25 ml dark rum
25 g butter, softened
1 tsp ground cinnamon

For the savoury filling
75 g tasty cheese, grated
½ small egg (from below)
15 g red onion,
  finely chopped
1 clove garlic, crushed
15 g finely chopped
  red capsicum
15 g finely chopped green
  capsicum
2 tbsp chopped fresh
  parsley
20 g sun-dried tomatoes,
  finely chopped
30 g pitted olives,
  chopped
½ tsp smoked
  ground paprika

For the scone dough
400 g plain flour
20 g caster sugar
25 g baking powder
a good pinch of salt
70 g butter, softened
1½ eggs (use other
  half above)
200 ml milk
1 tbsp water
additional flour, for dusting

V

METHOD

Sweet filling – mix all ingredients together in a bowl, ensuring that the dates are broken down a little; cover and set aside for a few hours or overnight, then mix again. You will notice the dates will break up easier as they soften, so the longer the soaking time the better.

Savoury filling – mix all ingredients together in a bowl to form a rough, spreadable paste. Cover and set aside until required.

Pre-heat the oven to 190–200°C.

Sift flour, sugar, baking powder and salt into a large mixing bowl. Add butter and rub in, using your fingertips and thumbs, to form coarse crumbs. Whisk 1 egg and the milk together and pour into the dry ingredients. Using a wooden spoon, mix together to form a soft dough. Tip dough onto a floured surface and knead for 10–20 seconds – don't over-knead or the dough will become too elastic.

Cut dough into two equal pieces and shape into squares. Using a rolling pin, roll out each dough piece on a floured surface to a 25 cm square.

Whisk the ½ egg and water together to make an egg wash.

Evenly spread one dough square with the sweet filling and the other with the savoury filling, leaving about 1 cm free along one edge of each. Brush egg wash along that edge.

Working towards the edge painted with egg wash, firmly roll up each dough sheet to achieve a Swiss roll or log shape. Using a large chef's knife or dough scraper, make a single lengthways cut along the middle of each log, right the way through.

For each log, take one strand in each hand, with the cut side of each strand facing towards you, and twist the strands around each other. Press the ends firmly together to make sure they do not unwind during the baking process. Place the twists on a baking tray lined with baking paper, keeping them well apart so they don't join together during baking. Brush the twists with the remaining egg wash and allow them to rest for 10 minutes.

Bake for 30–35 minutes. Halfway through the baking time, turn the tray to ensure an even colour. Remove from the oven and transfer to a cooling rack.

Masterton,
Wellington

AL BROWN MNZM
CHEF, RESTAURATEUR & AUTHOR

I'm a proud New Zealander and I'm proud to tell stories about the country through its food.

Food doesn't have to be perfect; it's people and place that create the memory and those are the special ingredients that make it taste so good.

A recipe is like a culinary love letter – you keep passing it on. Someone will take my recipe and add something to it and then it will become their recipe and then they will hopefully pass it on. My mum's ginger crunch will be passed on and who knows, in a couple of years' time, it might be being made in Canada or wherever; there's something inherently wonderful about that.

MUM'S GINGER CRUNCH

Recipe by *AL BROWN* MNZM, chef, restaurateur & author, Masterton, New Zealand

MAKES: 20 | **PREP TIME: 8 MINS** | **COOK TIME: 25 MINS PLUS SETTING** | **SKILL LEVEL: 1 (EASY)**

INGREDIENTS

Base
175 g butter
¾ cup sugar
1¼ cup plain flour
1½ tsp ground ginger
1½ tsp baking powder

Icing
100 g butter
1 cup icing sugar
2 tbsp golden syrup
4 tsp ground ginger

V

METHOD

Pre-heat the oven to 180°C. Grease and line a 25 cm x 20 cm baking tin. Cream butter and sugar together until pale. Sift in flour, ginger and baking powder and mix until combined. Press evenly into lined tin.

Bake for 20–25 minutes until base is firm to the touch. Remove from the oven and gently level out the base with the back of a spoon. Ice while the base is still warm.

Heat icing ingredients in a small saucepan. Stir until melted and combined. Pour the icing over the warm base and spread out evenly. Leave to cool in the tin before cutting into squares.

TIP

It is best to cut this slice in the tin, just before the icing is fully set, using a warm, wet knife.

JACOB BROWN
THE LARDER

There is a real sense of community here in Miramar. Our kids go to the local school and we have Weta Workshop just down the road. We get a lot of regulars here at The Larder, which we love.

One of the first things Sarah and I did when we first took over the building was cut a massive hole in the kitchen wall so we could connect with our customers. It's great to see friends walk past with their kids and be able to wave and say 'Hi'. I also think people appreciate seeing where their food comes from.

The only time it gets a bit awkward is when there is a queue of six people – and you go to say 'Hi' to one of them – and six people say 'Hi' and wave back! It's been really nice because, over time, many customers have become friends.

Jacob

Miramar,
Wellington

VENISON WELLINGTON WITH KALE

Recipes by *JACOB BROWN*, The Larder, Wellington, New Zealand

SERVINGS: 8 | PREP TIME: 1 HOUR | COOK TIME: 15 MINS | SKILL LEVEL: 2 (MODERATE)

INGREDIENTS

2 rashers streaky bacon
6 Portobello mushrooms
1 brown onion
1 clove garlic
1 tbsp butter
1¼ kg venison loin,
 trimmed and silver
 skin removed
20 ml vegetable oil
3 tbsp Dijon mustard
8 crêpes (see below)
square of puff pastry
 (45 cm x 45 cm)
4 egg yolks
2 tbsp cream
2 bunches fresh curly kale
butter, for cooking

METHOD

Cut bacon into 2 cm squares, de-stalk and slice mushrooms and thinly slice onion. Chop garlic. Sauté bacon in butter, over a medium heat, until golden-brown. Add onion and cook until soft. Add garlic and mushrooms, and cook until the liquid from the mushrooms has evaporated. Season with salt and pepper and set to one side.

Season venison with salt and pepper, then sear in oil in a heavy-based pan, over a high heat, to seal in the juices and caramelise the venison. Brush venison with Dijon mustard.

Spread crêpes out with them overlapping, to form a large mat. Place mushroom mix along the centre. Place Dijon-coated venison on top of the mushroom mix, and wrap the crêpes around the venison.

Mix together 2 egg yolks, brush puff pastry with egg yolk and place wrapped venison fillet in the centre. Roll the puff pastry over the venison fillet to fully encase it, pushing down on each side of the pastry to seal the venison inside the pastry. Glaze with egg wash made by combining remaining egg yolks with cream. Place the parcel on a baking tray lined with baking paper. (These steps can be done up to 24 hours in advance.)

When ready to cook, pre-heat the oven to 200°C and cook until the Wellington is golden-brown, approximately. 12–15 minutes. Leave to rest on a rack for 10 minutes, then slice with a sharp knife.

While the venison is resting, chop kale and gently sauté with a little butter, salt and pepper until wilted but still with a little bit of crunch. Serve venison on top of curly kale.

CRÊPES

SERVINGS: 8 | PREP TIME: 5 MINS PLUS RESTING | COOK TIME: 30 MINS | SKILL LEVEL: 1 (EASY)

INGREDIENTS

60 g plain flour
pinch of salt
50 g caster sugar
60 ml cream
1 egg
160 ml milk
15 ml melted butter
oil, for cooking

METHOD

Combine flour, salt and sugar in a bowl. In a separate bowl, beat together cream, egg and milk. Add this to the flour mixture, stirring with the whisk to combine. Leave the crêpe mix to sit for 1 hour, then add melted butter.

Heat a non-stick pan over medium heat. Lightly season pan with oil, then ladle in just enough batter to thinly coat the pan, tilting it to produce a uniformly thin crêpe. Cook over a moderate heat until bubbles appear on the surface of the crêpe. Gently flip the crêpe over and cook the other side until a pale golden colour. Remove the crêpe from the pan and repeat the process until all the crêpe batter has been used.

TIPS

Crêpes are delicious served with citrus yoghurt and fresh berries, or if you want something savoury try Gruyère and shavings of ham from the leg.

Melbourne, Victoria

GEORGE CALOMBARIS
CHEF, RESTAURATEUR & TV PRESENTER

My key food mantra is nostalgia. It's about putting smiles on people's faces.
Our past is what determines our future. We must always celebrate the present.
This is a simplified version of my restaurant's rice pudding. Measurements are
in grams as it is more precise when it comes to pastry making.

RISOGALO
GEORGE'S RICE PUDDING

Recipe by *GEORGE CALOMBARIS*, chef, restaurateur & TV presenter, Victoria, Australia

SERVINGS: 8 | PREP TIME: 1¾ HOURS | SKILL LEVEL: 3 (CHALLENGING)

INGREDIENTS

*For the rose water pastry
(makes 100 pieces approx.)*

125 g butter, at room
  temperature

½ tsp pure vanilla extract,
  or scraped-out seeds of
  1 vanilla bean

90 g sugar

1 egg

250 g standard flour

pinch of salt

½ cup sugar

½ cup water

1 tsp rose water

250 g icing sugar, sifted

*For the caramel sauce
(makes 200 g)*

100 ml cream

100 g sugar

pinch of salt (I use Murray
  River salt)

*For the rice pudding
(makes 2 cups)*

50 g risotto rice

500 ml milk

125 ml cream

zest of 1 lemon,
  and 10 ml juice

zest of ½ orange

1 small quill cinnamon

1 whole star anise

1 whole clove

75 g sugar

10 ml lemon juice

To assemble

2 large bananas

1 large block milk chocolate
  Aero, crushed into pieces

vanilla ice cream, to serve

METHOD

Rose water pastry: in an electric mixer, cream together the butter, vanilla and sugar until pale. Add the egg and combine. Remove the bowl from the mixer and fold through the flour and salt (it should look like breadcrumbs).

On a floured bench, knead the dough lightly until it forms a ball. Roll the pastry between two sheets of baking paper to a square about 15 cm x 15 cm and 3–5 mm thick. Place on a baking tray lined with baking paper, cover tray with plastic wrap and freeze for 30 minutes. Pre-heat the oven to 180°C fan-forced.

When firm, cut the frozen pastry into small squares, roughly 1 cm x 1 cm (don't worry if they're not completely uniform). Bake the squares for 10 minutes fan-forced, or until golden-brown.

Meanwhile, heat the sugar and water in a small saucepan over a medium heat until the sugar is dissolved. Remove from the heat and stir the rose water into the syrup until combined. Remove the hot pastry squares from the oven, quickly dip them into the rose water syrup and drain on a wire rack. Once cool, dust the squares with icing sugar and store in an airtight container until needed.

Caramel sauce: while the pastry is in the freezer, make the caramel sauce. Gently heat the cream in a small saucepan; set aside. Heat the sugar in a medium-sized, heavy-based, non-stick frying pan over a low to medium heat. Do not stir the sugar. Allow it to melt completely and turn amber in colour, being careful not to let it burn. This should take 8–12 minutes.

Stir the heated cream into the melted sugar until combined. Allow the caramel mixture to boil for 1 minute. Then add the salt, remove the pan from the heat, stir briefly and allow the caramel to rest for 10 minutes until cooled slightly. Strain the sauce through a mesh sieve and cool completely before serving.

Rice pudding: place the rice, milk, cream, half the lemon zest, all the orange zest, and the spices in a medium-sized, heavy-based saucepan over a medium heat and bring to the boil, stirring occasionally. Reduce the heat to low and add the sugar. Cook, stirring constantly, until one-third of the liquid has evaporated and the mixture has begun to thicken slightly. This should take approximately 30–40 minutes. Remove the rice pudding from the heat when the rice is soft and the sauce looks like custard. Remove the spices and stir in the remaining lemon zest and the lemon juice, until combined. Set aside until ready to serve.

To assemble: into eight ramekins or similar (½-cup capacity), spoon 2–4 tablespoons of warm rice pudding. Top each with 1–2 tablespoons caramel sauce, ¼ banana cut into thin slices, a few cubes of rose water pastry and a sprinkling of crushed Aero pieces. Serve with vanilla ice cream.

V

TORTILLA DE PATATAS

SPANISH OMELETTE

Recipe by *FRANK CAMORRA*, Movida, Victoria, Australia

SERVINGS: 4–6 | **PREP TIME: 30 MINS** | **COOK TIME: 10 MINS** | **SKILL LEVEL: 2 (MODERATE)**

INGREDIENTS

1¼ kg Désirée potatoes
1 large brown onion
1 litre olive oil, for cooking
12 large eggs
60 ml extra virgin olive oil,
  for frying

DF, GF, V

METHOD

Peel the potatoes and cut into 1 cm cubes, and dice onion. Heat the olive oil in a wide, deep heavy-bottomed pan over a medium heat until just warm, then add the potatoes and onions. Cook on a low to medium heat for 20 minutes. The oil should be just gently bubbling away, but not frying. When done, the potatoes will be soft but should not have gained any colour.

Break the eggs into a bowl and beat with a teaspoon of salt.

Drain the potatoes and onions, and season with salt. Allow to cool a little, then add to the eggs. Gently mix together.

In a 27 cm non-stick frying pan, heat pure olive oil over a high heat. When very hot, pour in the potato and egg mixture and mix well with a heatproof plastic spatula for 30 seconds.

Reduce heat to medium. Use the end of your spatula to break the potatoes up a little. Run the spatula around the side of the tortilla to form the edges. Cook for 3–4 minutes.

Cover the entire pan with a large plate and turn the tortilla over, then slide the uncooked side back into the hot pan. Keep cooking for 3–4 minutes on medium heat, with the plate acting as a lid.

The tortilla should be only lightly browned, and almost cooked through but slightly soft and moist in the centre. Once cooked, remove the plate that was acting as a lid. Place a clean plate on top that fits generously over the pan, then turn the pan over so that the tortilla sits on the plate. Cover with plastic wrap for 15 minutes to allow the latent heat to finish the cooking.

Slice and serve.

Wandsworth,
London

ANTONIO CARLUCCIO OBE, OMRI
CHEF & FOOD WRITER

I'm not a chef but a cook, and a cook loves passion and loves food and that's what I do. This stuffed olives recipe is one of my biggest specialities. You take the 'bone' out of an olive – a large olive – and then you replace it with a filling. Then you deep-fry it. It's a wonderful thing!

DEEP-FRIED STUFFED OLIVES

Recipe by *ANTONIO CARLUCCIO OBE, OMRI*, chef & food writer, London, England

MAKES: 50 | **PREP TIME: 30 MINS** | **COOK TIME: UP TO 1 HOUR** | **SKILL LEVEL: 2 (MODERATE)**

INGREDIENTS

For the filling

3 tbsp olive oil
50 g butter
100 g lean pork, finely minced
100 g lean veal, finely minced
50 g boneless chicken, minced
3 tbsp dry Marsala or sherry
1 small black truffle, diced
a few drops of truffle oil
30 g Parma ham, finely
  chopped
3 tbsp finely chopped parsley
½ tsp freshly grated nutmeg
finely grated zest of 1 lemon
1 egg, beaten
50 g Parmesan, freshly grated
a little milk (if needed)

50 Ascoli olives
olive oil, for deep-frying
plain white flour, for coating
2 eggs, beaten
dried breadcrumbs,
  for coating

METHOD

To make the filling, heat the olive oil and butter in a pan. Add the minced meats and fry, stirring, for 5–6 minutes until well browned. Season with salt and pepper, add the Marsala or sherry and allow to bubble to reduce down. Take off the heat and cool, then transfer to a food processor.

Add the truffle and truffle oil, Parma ham, parsley, nutmeg and lemon zest. Process briefly to mix, then add the egg and grated Parmesan, and whizz to combine. The mixture should be firm enough to use as a stuffing but not too dry; soften with a drop or two of milk if necessary.

Starting from the top, cut each olive in a spiral fashion to reach and release the stone inside, keeping the spiral intact. Take a little of the filling and enclose it in the olive spiral, pressing a little to regain the original shape.

Finish and cook the olives a few at a time. Heat the olive oil for deep-frying, in a suitable pan, to 180°C. Dip the olives in a little flour, then into the beaten egg, and then roll them in the breadcrumbs. Deep-fry for 2–3 minutes until brown, then drain on kitchen paper. Serve hot as an antipasto, with little lemon wedges if you like.

ANNA DEL CONTE OMRI
FOOD WRITER

Cooking Italian food is fundamentally
about buying the best ingredients and
cooking them with great simplicity,
without altering or trying to distract
from the flavour of the ingredient,
but just enhancing it with a little bit
of flavouring – although not too much.
It's more about what you leave out,
than what you put in!

Anna

*Shaftesbury,
Dorset*

ROTOLO DI SPINACI AL BURRO E FORMAGGIO
SPINACH & PASTA ROLL WITH MELTED BUTTER & PARMESAN

Recipe by *ANNA DEL CONTE*, food writer, Dorset, England

SERVINGS: 6 | **PREP TIME: 45 MINS PLUS RESTING** | **COOK TIME: 1¼ HOURS**
SKILL LEVEL: 2 (MODERATE)

This is a lovely vegetarian dish consisting of a roll of homemade pasta stuffed with spinach and ricotta, the most traditional of all vegetarian pasta fillings. The pasta must be rolled out by hand, but it is not too difficult to handle, being made with only 2 eggs. I recommend adding a teaspoon of oil to the dough to make it easier to stretch and roll thin. For the same reason I also suggest making a dough you would roll out by machine.

INGREDIENTS

500 g baby spinach leaves or 1 kg fresh bunch spinach

2 tbsp shallots, finely chopped

150 g unsalted butter

300 g fresh ricotta

100 g freshly grated Parmesan

¼ tsp ground nutmeg

1 free-range egg yolk

2 cloves garlic, peeled and bruised

a small sprig of fresh sage

For the pasta

200 g Italian 00 flour

2 free-range eggs

1 tsp olive oil, for rolling the pasta

METHOD

If you are using bunch spinach, discard any wilted or discoloured leaves, the roots and the long stems. Wash very well in a basin in several changes of cold water. The baby leaves only need one wash. Cook with just the water that clings to the leaves in a covered pan with sea salt until tender, then drain. Squeeze the spinach lightly in your hands to remove most of the moisture. Set aside.

In a frying pan, sauté the shallot with 45 grams of the butter over a medium heat. Chop the spinach coarsely by hand and when the shallot turns pale gold in colour, add it to the pan. Sauté for 5 minutes, turning the spinach over and over to insaporire – take up the flavour. You will find that all the butter has been absorbed.

Transfer the contents of the frying pan to a mixing bowl, and add the ricotta, half the grated Parmesan, the nutmeg, and, last of all, the egg yolk. Mix all the ingredients with a fork until they are all well blended. Taste and check seasoning.

Make the pasta dough. Put the flour on the work surface and make a well in the centre. Break the eggs into the well. Beat them lightly with a fork and draw the flour in gradually from the inner wall of the well. When the eggs are no longer runny, draw in enough flour to enable you to knead the dough with your hands. You may not need all the flour; push some to the side and add only what is needed. Alternatively you might need a little more from the bag, which you should keep at hand. Work until the flour and eggs are thoroughly amalgamated and then put the dough to one side and scrape the worktop clean.

Proceed to knead the dough by pressing and pushing with the heel of your palm, folding it back, giving it half a turn and repeating these movements. Repeat the movements for about 7–8 minutes. Wrap the dough in clingfilm and let it rest for at least 30 minutes, though you can leave it for up to 3 hours.

Roll out a rectangle of roughly 30 cm x 25 cm. Spread the filling over the pasta, starting about 5 cm in from the edge near you. The filling should cover all but a 5 mm border all round the sheet, and a larger border near you. Fold this border over the filling, and continue to fold until you have rolled up all the pasta. Wrap the pasta roll tightly in muslin, tying the two ends securely with string.

Use a fish kettle or other long, deep pan that can hold the roll and 3–4 litres of water. Bring the water to the boil, add 1 tablespoon of salt, then put in the pasta roll and cook at a gentle but steady simmer for 25 minutes after the water has come back to the boil. Lift the roll out, using the fish retriever in the kettle or two fish slices, and place on a wooden board. Unwrap the roll as soon as you can without burning your hands and set aside to cool a little, which will make slicing easier.

Pre-heat the oven to 200°C.

Cut the roll into 1 cm slices. Generously butter a large oven dish and lay the slices on it, overlapping a little.

Heat the remaining butter in a heavy frying pan with the garlic cloves and the sage. When the butter begins to turn a lovely golden colour, draw it off the heat. Remove and discard the garlic and the sage and then spoon the sauce evenly over the roll.

Cover the dish with foil and place in the oven until the roll is hot – about 10–20 minutes, depending on how hot it was when it went into the oven. Remove the dish from the oven and uncover it. Serve, handing the remaining Parmesan round separately.

TIPS

The rotolo can be made up to 2 days in advance and refrigerated, wrapped in foil.

Once cooked, allow the rotolo to cool, if you have time, because like any other food it becomes easier to slice. I use an electric carving knife, which I find one of the most useful tools. It is invaluable for slicing a roulade like this, or a stuffed fish, or a piece of braised meat that would otherwise tend to crumble.

After experimenting with different sauces to serve with the rotolo, I have come to the conclusion that the best, as so often, is the simplest: melted butter and Parmesan.

CLAYTON DONOVAN
INDIGENOUS CHEF & RESTAURATEUR

The women in my family form a huge part of what I know about my culture and I've passed what I know onto my kids. It's important that Australians know and consume our indigenous foods. Not only are they sustainable, but who knows what we'll also discover the more we pay attention. *Clayton*

Nambucca Heads,
New South Wales

OYSTERS WITH FINGER LIME, CARROT FOAM & AVOCADO CREAM

Recipe by *CLAYTON DONOVAN*, indigenous chef & restaurateur, New South Wales, Australia

SERVINGS: 2 | PREP TIME: 30 MINS | SKILL LEVEL: 2 (MODERATE)

INGREDIENTS

200 ml carrot juice
  (from about 6 carrots)
1½ tsp lecithin
2 avocados
2 tbsp lemon juice
100 ml cream
2 finger limes
12 shucked Nambucca
  River oysters

DF, GF

METHOD

Warm the carrot juice to blood temperature, and remove from the stove. Add the lecithin and stir. Season to taste with salt and pepper. Set aside.

Mash the avocados with the lemon juice. Push the mixture through a sieve. Whip the cream just under soft-peak stage. Fold the cream into the avocado mixture, then season to taste.

Squeeze out the liquid from the finger limes and remove the seeds.

Lightly pulse the carrot mixture until foam rises, then put aside to settle.

Place the avocado mixture on top of each oyster. Put the finger limes on top, then spoon the carrot foam on top of this.

RODNEY DUNN
THE AGRARIAN KITCHEN

Everything I do revolves around the seasons.
I love apples and grew up with apple crumble,
which was what Mum used to make and is
probably my all-time favourite. If I had a birthday,
the old apple crumble would be my choice. So
it was something that naturally came to mind
when I was thinking of something that is dear
to me and is very Australian.

Rodney

Lachlan,
Tasmania

APPLE & BERRY CRUMBLE WITH VANILLA CUSTARD

Recipe by *RODNEY DUNN*, The Agrarian Kitchen, Tasmania, Australia

SERVINGS: 6 | **PREP TIME: 40 MINS** | **COOK TIME: 35–40 MINS** | **SKILL LEVEL: I (EASY)**

INGREDIENTS

1½ kg apples
275 g sugar
1 vanilla bean,
  split lengthways
1½ cups raspberries

For the vanilla custard
500 ml milk
400 ml cream
1 vanilla bean,
  split lengthways
240 g egg yolk
  (from about 10 eggs)
200 g caster sugar

For the crumble mixture
150 g plain flour
120 g cold butter,
  finely chopped
90 g raw sugar
pinch of salt
50 g flaked almonds

V

METHOD

Peel and core apples and cut into 2 cm pieces. Place in a large saucepan with sugar and vanilla, cover and cook over a medium heat, stirring occasionally, until apples are soft and have broken apart; about 15–20 minutes. Remove from heat, add raspberries and carefully fold through. Remove vanilla bean and discard.

For vanilla custard: combine milk, cream and vanilla bean in a large saucepan and bring to the boil over a medium–high heat. Place egg yolks and sugar in a bowl, whisk until just combined, then gradually pour hot milk mixture into the bowl and whisk to combine. Return mixture to the same saucepan and stir over a low heat until mixture reaches 83°C; it will thicken enough to coat the back of a wooden spoon. Do not boil. Remove vanilla bean, scrape out seeds and stir seeds through custard.

For crumble mixture: place flour, butter, sugar and salt in a bowl and use your fingertips to rub the ingredients together, then mix almonds through.

Pre-heat oven to 200°C. Spoon apple and raspberry mixture into six ovenproof ramekins or one large ovenproof dish. Scatter with crumble mixture and place in the oven. Cook until the crumble is golden-brown and the mixture is beginning to bubble up the sides; 35–40 minutes.

Serve with vanilla custard.

ERRIEDA DU TOIT
CHEF, FOOD WRITER & TV PRESENTER

A lifetime is not enough to discover the diversity, the flavours and the history of food in this country. I try to take food from the past and bring it into modern times without losing those aspects that make the dish so well-loved and unique.

Errieda

*Welgemoed,
Western Cape*

MACARONI CHEESE WITH ROASTED TOMATOES

Recipe by *ERRIEDA DU TOIT*, chef, food writer & TV presenter, Western Cape, South Africa

SERVINGS: 6 | PREP TIME: 5 MINS | COOK TIME: 40 MINS | SKILL LEVEL: 1 (EASY)

INGREDIENTS

500 g macaroni

40 g butter

40 g flour

2–3 cloves garlic, crushed (optional)

750 ml warm milk

5 g mustard

250 g grated Cheddar

freshly grated nutmeg

12 'Rosa' or cherry tomatoes, cut into thick slices or halved

75 g cubed mozzarella for topping

about 50 g cubed leftover bread for topping

V

METHOD

Pre-heat the oven to 180°C. Bring a large pot of water to the boil, add the macaroni and cook until almost done, then drain.

In a medium saucepan, melt the butter, stir in the flour and add the garlic. Simmer gently till the garlic is soft and somewhat caramelised, not browned. Add half the milk, whisk until smooth, then add the rest and simmer till thickened and very smooth. Remove from the heat and stir in the mustard and half the Cheddar. Season with freshly grated nutmeg and plenty of salt and pepper.

Pour the cheese sauce over the pasta, stir well and put in a baking dish. Top with the rest of the grated Cheddar. Arrange the tomatoes, mozzarella cubes and bread cubes on top.

Bake in the oven until bubbly and golden-brown (about 20 minutes). The tomatoes must start to 'catch' and have slightly burnt edges.

JOSH EMETT
CHEF & RESTAURATEUR

I have blissful memories of life growing up
on the farm, running around doing whatever
we wanted and having animals everywhere.
In time, I grew to have a bit of respect for
the rabbits and wanted to do more than
just shoot them. This is a lovely easy dish
with classic flavours: essentially a rabbit
stew – it's a one-pot wonder!

Hamilton,
Waikato

AGRIA POTATO & CELERIAC GRATIN

Recipes by *JOSH EMETT*, chef & restaurateur, Waikato, New Zealand

SERVINGS: 4 | **PREP TIME: 15 MINS** | **COOK TIME: 30–40 MINS** | **SKILL LEVEL: 1 (EASY)**

INGREDIENTS

3 cloves garlic
2 large Agria potatoes
1 large celeriac
50 g Gruyère cheese
200 ml cream
200 ml milk

GF, V

METHOD

Pre-heat the oven to 180°C. Finely slice garlic, potatoes and celeriac (2 mm slices for the potato and celeriac). Grate cheese.

Place garlic, cream and milk in a pan and bring to the boil. Remove from heat and add potato and celeriac. Bring back to the boil, then remove from heat again.

Take an ovenproof dish and layer some potato and celeriac on the base, then top with cheese. Repeat to fill the dish, finishing with cheese. Pour the milk and cream mixture over to cover the potato and celeriac. Bake uncovered for 35–40 minutes until golden and potato is cooked through.

RABBIT CASSEROLE WITH BRANDY & PRUNES

SERVINGS: 6 | **PREP TIME: 40 MINS** | **COOK TIME: 30–40 MINS** | **SKILL LEVEL: 1 (EASY)**

INGREDIENTS

225 g shallots, peeled
3 cloves garlic, peeled
150 g carrots, sliced
100 g button mushrooms, halved
2 tbsp rice bran oil
1 large rabbit, cut into pieces
50 ml brandy
100 ml riesling
1 cinnamon quill
2 star anise
2 bay leaves
12 g fresh ginger, peeled and sliced
400 ml veal stock
250 g chicken stock
12 prunes

DF

METHOD

In a large casserole pot, sweat down shallots, garlic, carrots and mushrooms in oil until they pick up a little colour. Add rabbit pieces and lightly colour. Add brandy and reduce by half, then add riesling and also reduce by half. Add cinnamon, star anise, bay leaves, ginger and both stocks.

Bring to a simmer and skim. Lastly, add prunes then cover with a cartouche (greaseproof paper folded and torn to the same size as the pot) and continue to simmer slowly for 30–40 minutes until the rabbit is tender.

GIZZI ERSKINE
CHEF & TV PRESENTER

When you come round to my house, stuff is plonked on the table; you're sitting elbow to elbow, with carafes of wine, and we're all serving each other.

Food should be like that too, stepping away from everything that's a bit too fussy and just getting down to the nitty-gritty!

Bethnal Green,
London

WALNUT BAGNA CÀUDA

Recipe by *GIZZI ERSKINE*, chef & TV presenter, London, England

SERVINGS: 6 | **PREP TIME: 10 MINS** | **COOK TIME: 10 MINS** | **SKILL LEVEL: 1 (EASY)**

This is a recipe for which I have been searching for years. I first tried it at the famous London Italian restaurant San Lorenzo, and it has stuck with me forever. Traditionally bagna càuda is made as an oil- and butter-based dipping sauce, but my mum and I remember it being very walnutty. I researched the recipe and couldn't find a version with walnuts in it anywhere, but I did find some versions using walnut oil. I've totally made up this recipe, but it's pretty damn close to the original and, more importantly, it's delicious.

INGREDIENTS

150 ml extra virgin olive oil
3–4 cloves garlic, finely
    chopped
8 anchovies
100 g walnuts
150 ml double cream
30 g butter
30 ml walnut oil
1 tsp lemon juice
crudités (such as baby
    fennel, artichokes,
    carrots and radishes)

METHOD

Heat the olive oil in a saucepan, then add the garlic and fry it very slowly in the oil for about 1–2 minutes, or until the garlic has tinged a little golden. Add the anchovies and let them melt away into the oil. Next, add the walnuts and gently toast them for 1 minute. Add the double cream and butter and cook for 2 minutes, or until the mixture is piping hot, and then finish with the walnut oil and lemon juice.

Now you need to blend this to a purée in a small blender. You want it to be the texture of a thin, creamy hummus, almost like a thick, coating-consistency salad dressing. Transfer the bagna càuda to a heatproof pot with a flame underneath (the obvious choice would be a fondue pot) and plunge away at it with your crudités.

COLIN FASSNIDGE
FOUR IN HAND

Our trick at home with feeding the kids is to find
out what they like that's healthy – then we just
pound it into them!

Matraville,
New South Wales

SALAD OF WATERMELON, FENNEL, PEAS & FETA

Recipe by *COLIN FASSNIDGE*, Four in Hand, New South Wales, Australia

SERVINGS: 4 | PREP TIME: 15 MINS | SKILL LEVEL: 1 (EASY)

INGREDIENTS

½ large watermelon
2 baby fennel
1 cup creamy-style feta
1 cup shelled garden peas
  (defrosted baby peas
  also work)
½ bunch mint,
  leaves picked
good-quality olive oil

GF, V

METHOD

Cut watermelon flesh into bite-sized chunks. Shave or finely slice the fennel, and gently crumble the feta.

In a salad bowl, combine the watermelon, fennel, feta, peas and mint. Dress with a drizzle of olive oil and salt and pepper to taste.

SKYE FEHLMANN
NATURALLY ORGANIC

For me, food is soil, and soil is the lifeblood of good food.
Nourishing the soil is a large part of what we do on the farm —
compost is king! I started farming organically when I realised
I was eating food that was damaging nature, the world and,
in effect, us as humans. Our land is constantly under threat
as the city sprawls, so a big part of what we do is educating
people about the importance of the land as a food source.

*Philippi,
Western Cape*

BRAAIED ZUCCHINI WITH TORTILLAS & PESTO

Recipe by *SKYE FEHLMANN*, Naturally Organic, Western Cape, South Africa

SERVINGS: 4 | PREP TIME: 10 MINS | COOK TIME: 15 MINS | SKILL LEVEL: 1 (EASY)

INGREDIENTS

6 zucchini, sliced in half
  lengthways

olive oil

12 corn tortillas
  (I use non-GMO)

3 balls mozzarella, torn

1 cup homemade basil pesto
  (see recipe page 316)

250 g sour cream or crème
  fraîche

green leaves, to serve

edible flowers, to serve

GF, V

METHOD

In a large bowl, toss the zucchini slices with olive oil and season really well with salt and pepper. Once the braai coals are ready, grill the zucchini for a few minutes on each side until just cooked through (a little crunch is good). Remove from heat and set aside. Heat the tortillas on the braai for a few minutes on each side. Serve the warm tortillas stuffed with the braaied zucchini and torn mozzarella, plus dollops of pesto and sour cream, green leaves and edible flowers.

TUI FLOWER
COOK & FOOD WRITER

One of the earliest memories of learning
to cook is helping to make this raisin loaf.
I wondered if I would ever know how
to judge when the oven was the right
temperature to bake it. I watched as my
mother held the handle of the oven door
on the coal range or opened the door
and held her hand in the oven briefly.
This easy, modest, good-keeping loaf
has been a staple throughout my life.

Tui

*Mt Eden,
Auckland*

RAISIN LOAF

Recipes by *TUI FLOWER*, cook & food writer, Auckland, New Zealand

SERVINGS: 8 | **PREP TIME: 15 MINS** | **COOK TIME: 1 HOUR** | **SKILL LEVEL: 1 (EASY)**

INGREDIENTS

1 cup milk
2 tbsp golden syrup
2 cups plain flour
3 tsp baking powder
pinch of salt
¾ cup sugar
1 cup raisins

V

METHOD

Pre-heat the oven to 180°C. Line the bottom of a 22 cm loaf tin with baking paper and grease the tin.

Put milk and golden syrup together in a pan and heat gently to combine. Leave to cool. Sift flour, baking powder and salt into a bowl, add sugar and raisins and stir to combine. Add the milk mixture, stirring to make a soft batter. Turn into the prepared tin.

Bake for about 1 hour. Allow to cool in the tin for 15–20 minutes, before removing to cool completely. Serve sliced, with or without buttering.

TIP

This is a forgiving recipe, so if you find measuring golden syrup tricky, a little inaccuracy will be allowed. It will also tolerate milk starting to sour.

MARGARET FULTON OAM, COOK & AUTHOR
& SUZANNE GIBBS, COOK & FOOD WRITER

All of us Fulton women have fond memories of being happy in the kitchen and I think children should be introduced to the kitchen at a very early age. Even the smallest member of the family can have a job, even if it's just shelling peas. Children who grow up in the kitchen and slowly learn to cook enjoy growing up learning the simple joy of appreciation for this effort. It makes you feel good as a young person... and a not-so-young person, too!

margaret Fulton

Balmain,
New South Wales

HONEY SPICE ROLL

Recipe by *MARGARET FULTON OAM*, cook & author
& *SUZANNE GIBBS*, cook & food writer, New South Wales, Australia

SERVINGS: 6–8 | **PREP TIME: 30 MINS** | **COOK TIME: 20 MINS** | **SKILL LEVEL: 1 (EASY)**

INGREDIENTS

4 eggs, separated
½ cup (110 g) caster sugar,
  plus 1 tbsp
  extra to dust
½ cup (75 g) cornflour
3 tbsp plain flour
3 tsp baking powder
1 tsp mixed spice
½ tsp ground cinnamon
¼ cup liquid honey,
  at room temperature
180 ml thickened cream

V

METHOD

Pre-heat the oven to 180°C (or 160°C fan-forced). Lightly grease and line the base and sides of a 23 cm x 32 cm Swiss roll tin.

Using an electric mixer, beat egg whites until firm but not dry. Add the ½ cup of sugar, 1 tbsp at a time, beating constantly until mixture is thick and glossy. Beat in egg yolks until just combined.

Sift together cornflour, flour, baking powder, mixed spice and cinnamon. Lightly foldinto egg mixture with 1 tbsp of honey, until evenly distributed. Fill prepared tin, shaking gently to spread mixture evenly.

Bake for 20 minutes, until sponge springs back when lightly touched. Turn out onto a tea towel lightly dusted with extra caster sugar. Peel off paper and trim edges. Roll sponge up immediately in a tea towel, starting from a short edge. Set aside to cool.

Whip cream with remaining honey. Unroll cake and spread cream over. Roll up again and cover with plastic wrap. Chill in the fridge for 30 minutes, then cut into slices to serve.

CLASSIC SPONGE CAKE

Recipe by *MARGARET FULTON OAM*, cook & author
& *SUZANNE GIBBS*, cook & food writer, New South Wales, Australia

SERVINGS: 6–8 | PREP TIME: 20 MINS | COOK TIME: 30 MINS | SKILL LEVEL: 1 (EASY)

INGREDIENTS

95 g self-raising flour
25 g cornflour
4 eggs, separated
100 g caster sugar,
  plus 2 tbsp extra
1 tsp vanilla extract
¼ tsp cream of tartar
300 ml cream, whipped
1 punnet strawberries,
  hulled and sliced, to fill
icing sugar, to dust

V

METHOD

Pre-heat the oven to 200°C. Grease and line the base of a 22 cm cake tin. Sift the flour and cornflour together, and set aside.

Using an electric mixer, whisk together egg yolks, the 100 grams of caster sugar and vanilla for 2–3 minutes, until thick and mousse-like. Set aside.

Whisk egg whites until starting to froth, then add cream of tartar and continue to whisk until stiff but not dry. Whisk in the 2 tablespoons of sugar gradually.

Fold a large scoop of whisked egg white into the beaten yolks, to slacken the mixture, then fold in the sifted flour and finally the remaining egg whites, until just combined.

Turn the mixture into the prepared tin, gently smoothing the top. Place in the oven, reducing the temperature to 170°C, and bake for 30 minutes. Check if the cake is cooked before taking it out of the oven by very gently pressing with an index finger to check if the centre of the cake is firm. If so, remove from the oven and check the centre with a very fine cake skewer – it should come out clean. Leave to cool in the tin for 5 minutes before removing to cool completely on a wire rack, to make sure the top is nicely set.

Once cooled, split the cake by cutting with a sharp serrated knife into two even rounds. Top the base with whipped cream and strawberries, then place the cake top on.

When ready to serve, dust with icing sugar.

TIP

Instead of splitting one sponge, this classic cake can be made by baking two sponges and sandwiching them with the cream and strawberries.

SIMON GAULT
CHEF & RESTAURATEUR

I have early memories of my dad going snorkling around the wharf and rocks at Paihia, looking for mussels. We'd take them home, steam them open on the barbecue and then eat them, just like that. Green-lipped mussels are New Zealand seafood heroes and by adding a touch of cheese, pulling all those tough bits out and not overcooking them, you end up with a fritter that says New Zealand, says unique and says damned good.

Simon

Drury,
Auckland

MUSSEL FRITTERS

Recipe by *SIMON GAULT*, chef & restaurateur, Auckland, New Zealand

SERVINGS: 4–6 | PREP TIME: 30 MINS | COOK TIME: 20 MINS | SKILL LEVEL: 2 (MODERATE)

INGREDIENTS

600 g mussel meat (about 3½ kg fresh mussels)

100 ml white wine

100 g mascarpone

zest of 1 lemon

20 ml lemon juice

250 g Parmesan

160 g finely chopped onion

2 cups flour

2 tsp salt

2 tsp baking powder

½ tsp freshly ground black pepper

4 eggs

1 cup milk

50 ml extra virgin olive oil

2 tbsp capers

100 ml canola oil

fresh pea tendrils to garnish

METHOD

Clean mussels thoroughly and place them in a saucepan with wine. Cover and bring to a simmer. With a spoon, rotate mussels in the wine. As the shells open, remove them from the saucepan and allow to cool. Discard any mussels that don't open. To de-beard your mussels, pull the threads down towards the pointy end of the shell, discarding the brown foot and any muscle attached to the shell. Remove mussel meat from the shells, then remove tongues and the main (round) muscle. Cut mussels into halves or thirds depending on size.

In a small bowl, mix mascarpone, lemon zest and juice together and set aside until required. Grate Parmesan and chop onion.

Put flour, salt, baking powder and pepper in a bowl and mix together. Add eggs and milk to create a thick batter, and then add Parmesan, onion and mussel meat. Mix through the batter.

In a non-stick pan, heat a splash of olive oil until hot and add a generous spoonful of batter for each fritter. Cook until golden-brown on both sides and firm to the touch. Repeat until all the batter is cooked. Keep warm or reheat in a microwave before serving.

If capers are salted, soak in water for about 10 minutes. Heat canola oil until it shimmers and fry capers until crispy. Remove and drain on paper towels. Place fritters on a board draped with baking paper, and serve with a heaped tablespoonful of mascarpone mix and sprinkled with fried capers. Garnish with pea tendrils.

PETER GILMORE
QUAY

This Korean chicken soup became a family favourite
to cook on Sunday nights at home, and sometimes
I like to make it at Quay. When you have a really
stressful, busy day, the staff meal is something that
everyone looks forward to, and something comforting
like this soup gives you 10 minutes out of your day.
For me, it makes me feel like I'm home and then we
get back into work.

Peter Gilmore

The Rocks,
New South Wales

KOREAN CHICKEN SOUP

Recipe by *PETER GILMORE*, Quay, New South Wales, Australia

SERVINGS: 6 | PREP TIME: 30 MINS | COOK TIME: 1½ HOURS | SKILL LEVEL: 1 (EASY)

INGREDIENTS

1¾ kg whole free-range chicken

2½ litres cold water

100 g unsalted butter

2 tbsp Korean sesame oil

2 medium onions, roughly diced

1 small knob fresh ginger, finely sliced

3 cloves garlic, finely diced

100 g fresh shiitake mushrooms, finely sliced

150 g fresh oyster mushrooms, torn into thirds

3 tsp mild Korean chilli flakes

2 tbsp fish sauce

2 tbsp light soy sauce

300 g chopped kimchi (available from Asian supermarkets)

400 g thin somen wheat noodles

1 small bunch baby bok choy, finely sliced

5 Asian green spring onions, white part only, finely sliced

2 tbsp fresh lime juice

2 free-range eggs, beaten

3 tbsp toasted sesame seeds, for garnish

DF

METHOD

Place the chicken in a large saucepan with the cold water. Bring the chicken and water just to boiling point, then reduce to a low simmer for 30 minutes. Carefully remove the chicken with a pair of tongs and a spoon and place into a colander. Allow the chicken to cool for 15 minutes.

Wearing gloves, remove the leg, thigh and breast meat. Return all the chicken bones and carcass to the cooking liquid and continue to simmer on low for a further 30 minutes. Chop the cooled chicken meat into small pieces and place in the refrigerator.

To a separate clean saucepan, add the butter and sesame oil and place on a medium heat. Add the onion and sweat for 2 minutes. Add the ginger and garlic and sweat for a further minute. Add the shiitake and oyster mushrooms and sweat for 2 minutes. Add the chilli flakes, fish sauce, soy sauce and kimchi. Stir and remove from the heat.

Use a ladle to remove any impurities and fat from the surface of the chicken stock. Pass the stock through a fine sieve and add it to the pan of vegetables. Simmer soup on low for 20 minutes.

Bring a separate pan of water to the boil, add the somen noodles and cook for 2 minutes. Drain the noodles and divide equally between six warmed bowls. Turn the soup up to high, add the chicken meat, bok choy, spring onions and lime juice. As soon as the soup starts to boil, turn off the heat. Taste the soup and correct the seasoning with sea salt if necessary. Stir the soup to create a whirlpool, then add the beaten egg. Serve a generous ladleful of soup on top of the warm noodles and garnish with toasted sesame seeds.

PETER GORDON ONZM
CHEF & RESTAURATEUR

When I think back to my childhood in Whanganui,
the dish that most stands out is Dad's soufflé omelette.
Bruce is your typical Kiwi bloke – so where he conceived
of the idea to beat egg whites into an omelette escapes
me. And him, actually!

Pete

Whanganui,
Manawatu-Whanganui

BRUCE GORDON'S SOUFFLÉ OMELETTE

Recipe by *PETER GORDON* ONZM, chef & restaurateur, Manawatu-Whanganui, New Zealand

SERVINGS: 4 | **PREP TIME: 5 MINS** | **COOK TIME: 20 MINS** | **SKILL LEVEL: 1 (EASY)**

INGREDIENTS

½ large onion
  (I use a red one)
2 tomatoes
6 rashers smoked
  streaky bacon
6 eggs
a few knobs of butter
2 tbsp grated Cheddar

GF

METHOD

Dice onion and tomatoes, and cut bacon into lardons. Separate eggs into two largish bowls. Turn the oven grill on.

Heat some butter in a frying pan over medium heat until sizzling. Add onion and cook until beginning to caramelise, stirring often. Add bacon and cook until it begins to crisp up a little. Add tomatoes and cook for a few minutes until any extra moisture is evaporated, stirring.

Meanwhile, beat egg whites with a pinch of salt until thick and foamy.

Tip bacon mixture onto yolks and mix together well. Fold beaten whites into egg yolk mixture.

Put the pan back on the heat and add a knob of butter. Once butter is sizzling, tip omelette mixture back into the pan and put a lid on. Cook over low–medium heat for 3 minutes, until the whites firm up a little.

Take the lid off, sprinkle with cheese and place under the grill. Once golden and bubbling, remove the pan from the heat and cut into four. Serve on buttered toast.

NIKKI & DOUG GOVAN
STAR OF GREECE

Sunset is unbeatable.

And even in the middle of winter, looking out to the storms and waves, it's always fantastic to look out over the water.

We like to sit on the deck having a glass of wine and watching the sun sink into the ocean.

Whether we're with family or it's just the two of us, it's peaceful and a very nice place to be. *Nikki & Doug*

*Port Willunga,
South Australia*

SALT & PEPPER SQUID WITH LEMON & GARLIC MAYO

Recipes by *NIKKI & DOUG GOVAN*, Star of Greece, South Australia, Australia

SERVINGS: 5 | PREP TIME: 20 MINS | SKILL LEVEL: 2 (MODERATE)

INGREDIENTS

Lemon and garlic mayo
2 whole eggs
2 egg yolks
1 tsp Dijon mustard
½ tsp minced garlic
400 ml olive oil
juice of 1 lemon

oil, for deep-frying
2 whole fresh squid
1 bottle soda water
250 g coarse rice flour

DF, GF

METHOD

Make the lemon and garlic mayo by blending eggs, yolks, mustard and garlic in an electric mixer until creamy and light. Slowly and steadily beat in olive oil. Once combined, mix in lemon juice and set aside.

Heat oil in a deep-fryer to 180°C.

Clean the squid by cutting the tentacles off the body; reserve the tentacles. Pull the head, guts and feather out of the squid tube in one motion, and discard. Clean the squid tube by scraping the membrane away from the flesh, keeping the wings on the body. Slice the tube into rings about 1 cm thick and add to the tentacles.

Wash squid with soda water, then drain in a colander. Once drained, toss squid in rice flour, shake off extra flour and deep-fry for about 30–40 seconds. Toss squid with sea salt and freshly ground black pepper to taste, and serve with the lemon and garlic mayo.

ALE-BATTERED KING GEORGE WHITING WITH HAND-CUT CHIPS

SERVINGS: 4 | PREP TIME: 5 MINS | COOK TIME: 30 MINS PLUS CHILLING | SKILL LEVEL: 1 (EASY)

INGREDIENTS

For the hand-cut chips
oil, for deep-frying
8 medium-sized Désirée
  potatoes

For the fish
oil for deep-frying
8 fillets King George
  whiting (or any
  other delicate
  white-fleshed fish)
225 g self-raising flour
1 bottle sparkling ale
  (we use Coopers)
plain flour, to coat

DF

METHOD

Heat oil to 180°C in a deep-fryer.

Slice potatoes lengthways into eighths. Plunge them, all at once, into the hot oil in the deep-fryer and immediately turn the temperature down to 120°C. Cook for 10–15 minutes or until chips are cooked but still firm. Spread out on a large tray and cool in the fridge. Turn deep-fryer back up to 180°C.

Cut the fins off and pin-bones out from the whiting fillets.

To make the batter, slowly whisk the flour into the ale, whisking until you have a smooth batter.

When ready to cook, toss the fillets a few at a time in enough plain flour to coat. Dip the fillets into the batter and carefully lower them into the hot oil. The fish will float and needs to be turned over once the bottom side is a nice light-golden colour (this should take about 1 minute). Continue to fry until evenly coloured on that side, then remove fish and drain on a paper towel.

Fry chilled chips at 180°C until golden and crisp. Season with salt and serve with the fish.

SLAW WITH PEARS, TOASTED HAZELNUTS & BUTTERMILK DRESSING

Recipe by *SKYE GYNGELL*, Spring, London, England

SERVINGS: 6 | **PREP TIME: 15 MINS** | **COOK TIME: 5 MINS** | **SKILL LEVEL: 1 (EASY)**

There is nothing quite like a really good coleslaw. It makes for an excellent side, especially with grilled meats or rich, slow-cooked dishes such as shoulder of pork. It's easy to prepare and, unlike most salads, really benefits from being dressed a couple of hours in advance to allow time for the flavours to develop and mellow. You can add and subtract ingredients as you like, but I think this salad needs both a nutty crunch and a little fruity sweetness to make it really interesting. The dressing, which includes buttermilk and cider vinegar, gives it a creamy, yet gutsy, finish.

INGREDIENTS

120 g shelled and skinned hazelnuts

¼ red cabbage, cored

¼ white cabbage, cored

1 fennel bulb, peeled

3 firm ripe pears

a bunch of flat-leaf parsley, leaves only

For the dressing

1 organic free-range egg yolk

½ tbsp Dijon mustard

1½ tsp honey

1 tbsp good-quality cider vinegar

180 ml mild-tasting extra virgin olive oil

2 tbsp buttermilk

GF, V

METHOD

Pre-heat the oven to 180°C. Spread the hazelnuts out on a baking sheet and toast them on the middle shelf of the oven for 4–5 minutes. Remove from the oven and allow to cool, then chop roughly.

Finely slice both the red and the white cabbage into thin ribbons and place in a bowl. Remove the tough, fibrous outer layer from the fennel, cut the bulb in half lengthways and then slice very finely. Add to the cabbage.

Halve the pears, remove the cores and then slice finely. Add to the bowl of cabbage and fennel, toss lightly and season well with salt and plenty of black pepper. Set aside while you make the dressing.

Put the egg yolk, mustard, honey and vinegar into a small bowl. Season with a little salt and pepper and stir vigorously to combine. Now whisk in the olive oil slowly, almost drip by drip to begin with, increasing the flow slightly once the dressing begins to homogenise. Continue until all the oil is incorporated. Stir in the buttermilk, then taste and adjust the seasoning as necessary.

Pour the dressing over the salad with the hazelnuts and parsley and mix together gently but thoroughly using your fingertips. Set aside in a cool place for an hour or two before serving.

BRIGITTE HAFNER
GERTRUDE STREET ENOTECA

Italian food has been the strongest influence in my cooking life. I was really taken with how Italians approach cooking. How they are obsessive about slicing garlic and how you handle vegetables. They can make zucchini sing in a way I've never seen. Almost all of Italian food is very simple; it's about life and energy, which is how I like to cook.

Mornington Peninsula, Victoria

ABRUZZO-STYLE PORK STEW WITH ROASTED CAPSICUM, CHILLI & FENNEL

Recipe by *BRIGITTE HAFNER*, Gertrude Street Enoteca, Victoria, Australia

SERVINGS: 6 | PREP TIME: 45 MINS | COOK TIME: 1–1½ HOURS | SKILL LEVEL: 1 (EASY)

INGREDIENTS

1 kg pork shoulder, cut into 5 cm dice

3 tbsp extra virgin olive oil

70 g fatty pancetta

3 large cloves garlic

½ bunch parsley

1 tsp fennel seeds

⅓ cup medium-bodied white wine

½ tsp dried chilli flakes

1 x 400 g can Italian peeled tomatoes, chopped

2 red capsicums

1 tbsp sherry or red wine vinegar

½ tbsp white sugar

For the wet polenta

3 cups water

2 tsp salt

1½ cups fine yellow polenta

1 big knob butter

½ cup grated Parmesan

GF

METHOD

In a heavy-based pot such as a cast-iron casserole, brown the pork in the olive oil in small batches. Remove to a plate and sprinkle with salt. Remove the pot from the heat and allow to cool, but don't throw out the fat.

Cut the pancetta into very small pieces, then chop the garlic and parsley as well. Now, combine the pancetta, garlic, parsley and fennel seeds, and using a mezzaluna or a heavy knife, finely chop everything together until you have a fine paste. Add this paste to the pot over a low heat and cook, stirring all the time with a wooden spoon, until the paste becomes fragrant and the garlic turns golden-brown.

Add the pork and its juices back to the pot at once, with the wine and chilli flakes. Increase the heat and simmer for a few minutes, stirring to get the delicious brown stuff off the bottom of the pot and into the sauce. Now add the tomatoes. Reduce the heat to a very low and gentle simmer. Cover with a skewed lid and allow to cook until the pork is tender, about 1–1½ hours.

Pre-heat the oven to 220°C and roast the capsicums until blistered. Cool, peel and chop the flesh into small pieces.

For the wet polenta, bring the water and salt to the boil in a large pot, then add the polenta in a fine, steady stream while stirring with a whisk. Turn the heat to the lowest setting and simmer gently, stirring with a wooden spoon, until very thick (about 15 minutes). Add the butter and Parmesan and serve as soon as possible.

To finish, add the roasted capsicum, sherry or vinegar and sugar to the pork and season with salt if needed. Serve on the wet polenta.

CHIA SEED CHAI BUTTERNUT BREAKFAST PUDDING

Recipe by *MELISSA & JASMINE HEMSLEY*, food consultants, London, England

SERVINGS: 4 | PREP TIME: 20 MINS PLUS RESTING | COOK TIME: 55 MINS | SKILL LEVEL: 1 (EASY)

This is an overnight breakfast or make-ahead dessert. We've infused omega-3-rich chia seeds with our favourite rooibos chai breakfast tea and together they turn the usually savoury butternut squash into a sweet start to the day. This is so yummy that you'll also fancy it as a cool, creamy dessert. We love it with summer fruits, such as blackberries, grapes, figs, plums or peaches, which are just in season as butternut comes in. In the winter months, try apple chunks, chopped clementines or blood orange segments. If you bake the butternut squash the night before, then it's ready to go in the morning. Don't forget to chew well in order to get the most goodness out of the tiny chia seeds. We use white chia to keep the pudding's bright orange colour, but black also works — and is cheaper and easier to find, too!

INGREDIENTS

1 large butternut squash
(enough to make 400 g
cooked butternut squash
purée)

350 ml water

3 tbsp coconut oil

2 tsp rooibos chai tea
leaves, or 2 rooibos chai
tea bags

4 tbsp white chia seeds

1 tbsp raw honey

coconut yoghurt and goji
berries (optional), to serve

DF, GF, V

METHOD

Pre-heat the oven to 200°C and roast the butternut squash in the oven for 40–50 minutes until cooked through and tender. Scoop out 400 g of the squash flesh and mash well. Any leftover squash can be frozen and used in a soup or smoothie.

Add the squash to a saucepan with the water, coconut oil and the tea leaves or the contents of the tea bags. Bring to a medium simmer, then remove from the heat and leave to cool for a few minutes.

Stir in the chia seeds, continuously whisking at first to avoid lumps, then add the honey.

Leave to sit for at least 20 minutes to an hour for the chia to swell (unless you like it crunchy). Alternatively, transfer to a flask and by the time you get to work, you'll have a nice warm chia breakfast pudding.

Add the coconut yoghurt and goji berries, if using, and enjoy.

NICK HOLLOWAY
NU NU

Flavour is everywhere! It's in the bottom of the pan, in the last little scraps of vegetable. Being resourceful in the kitchen means you'll never throw any piece of food away and if you're a talented cook, the plates come back empty!

Nicko

Palm Cove,
Queensland

WOOD-ROASTED REEF FISH WITH PINEAPPLE CURRY

Recipe by *NICK HOLLOWAY*, Nu Nu, Queensland, Australia

SERVINGS: 4 | PREP TIME: 2 HOURS | COOK TIME: 1 HOUR | SKILL LEVEL: 2 (MODERATE))

INGREDIENTS

For the pineapple curry

5 large dried long red chillies, de-seeded and soaked in water for at least 1 hour, preferably overnight

4 tbsp roughly chopped garlic

5 tbsp roughly chopped red shallots

4 tbsp finely sliced lemongrass, tender inner part only

1 tbsp peeled and grated galangal

1 tbsp washed and scraped coriander roots

1 tbsp fresh turmeric

1 tsp good-quality Thai shrimp paste, roasted (see tip below)

DF, GF

3 tbsp coconut cream

1 tbsp ginger oil (see tip below)

2 kaffir lime leaves, bruised

1–2 tbsp pale palm sugar, crushed

1 cup fish stock

1 tbsp fish sauce (approx.) (start with 1 tsp and add more to taste)

½ pineapple, grated and juice collected

1 tbsp thick tamarind water (see tip below)

juice of 2 limes

For the fish

1 beautiful reef fish, 1¼–1½ kg (I like mine freshly line-caught and brain-spiked)

1 tbsp cane sugar

2 tbsp good-quality fish sauce

3 cups assorted coriander, Thai basil, Vietnamese mint and mint leaves

4 tsp fried garlic crisps

4 tbsp fried shallot crisps

2 kaffir lime leaves, finely sliced into threads

2 lemon leaves, finely sliced into threads

2 limes, sliced into thin rings

handful shaved coconut, toasted in a dry pan

METHOD

First make the pineapple curry. Grind the chilli, garlic, shallots, lemongrass, galangal, coriander roots, turmeric and shrimp paste with a pinch of salt in a food processor or mortar and pestle until very smooth and fine.

Crack coconut cream by simmering it in a heavy-based pot or wok until it splits into a curdled-looking substance. Add ginger oil then add the curry paste with the bruised kaffir lime leaves and fry over an even heat until heady and fragrant. It should take 10–15 minutes and smell beautifully perfumed.

Add the palm sugar and continue to fry for a few moments to caramelise the sugar and deepen the colour. Finally add the stock, fish sauce, grated pineapple and juice, and tamarind water, and bring the curry back to a gentle simmer for another 10 minutes to allow the flavours to coalesce.

Squeeze in the fresh lime juice and adjust the seasoning as necessary. The curry should taste rich, sour and slightly sweet and have a wonderful orange film of oil on top.

Remove and discard the scales, gills and guts from the fish. Score the fish with a sharp knife and then rub it with the sugar and fish sauce. Tuck the seasoned fish into a snug tray and allow it to marinate for 5–10 minutes.

Light a fire using your favourite wood and allow it to burn down to coals. Cook the fish in amongst the coals until it starts to colour, then pour over the prepared curry and simmer until the fish falls from the bone gracefully.

Scatter over the herbs, garlic and shallot crisps, leaf threads, sliced limes and toasted coconut and serve in the tray.

TIPS

To roast shrimp paste, spread the required quantity onto a double thickness of tinfoil and fold into a flat 'envelope' encasing the paste. Place the packet directly onto the coals or grill of a barbecue and roast for a few minutes each side. Cool.

For ginger oil, place several slices of fresh ginger in 100 ml vegetable oil and warm gently (to 50–60°C). The oil can be used straight away, but will mature further with time if you store it with the ginger left in.

Make tamarind water by breaking up tamarind pulp with your fingers in a little warm water and straining out the seeds.

PIKELETS

Recipe by DAME ALISON HOLST DNZM, CBE, QSM, cook & author, Auckland, New Zealand

SERVINGS: 4 | **PREP TIME: 4 MINS** | **COOK TIME: 15–20 MINS** | **SKILL LEVEL: 1 (EASY)**

My mother was a wonderful cook and I started cooking by helping her out in the kitchen. I have always loved teaching people to cook and encouraging them to produce interesting, tasty and varied meals without spending too much time and money. Cooking is not scary! Pikelets are simple, inexpensive food. They don't take very long to make and everybody likes them.

INGREDIENTS

1 rounded tbsp golden syrup
25 g butter
1 tbsp sugar
½ cup milk
1 large egg
1 cup self-raising flour

V

METHOD

Heat a frying pan. (Use a high heat setting if the frying pan is electric.) Dip an ordinary tablespoon in hot water and use to measure the golden syrup into a bowl. Add butter and warm to soften both (microwaving is easiest), then mix in sugar, milk and egg. Sprinkle or sieve flour over the top, then mix in briefly with a whisk or beater just until smooth.

Rub the surface of the hot frying pan with a little butter on a paper towel. Drop dessertspoon or tablespoon lots of mixture into the pan, pouring mixture off the tip of the spoon. If the mixture is too thick and doesn't spread easily, add a little extra milk to it.

Turn pikelets over as soon as bubbles begin to burst on the surface. (Turn heat up if the cooked sides are not brown enough OR turn heat down if they brown too much by the time the first bubbles burst.) Cook the second side until the centres spring back when touched with your finger.

Cook in batches until all the batter is used. Keep cooked pikelets warm between the folds of a clean tea towel. Serve soon after making – spread with butter and jam, top butter with hundreds and thousands for small children, or 'dress them up' with whipped cream, jam and fresh berries. Yum!

COQ AU VIN

CHICKEN BRAISED IN RED WINE

Recipe by *DIANE HOLUIGUE OAM*, The French Kitchen, Victoria, Australia

SERVINGS: 6 | **PREP TIME: 30 MINS** | **COOK TIME: 1¼ HOURS** | **SKILL LEVEL: 1 (EASY)**

INGREDIENTS

60 g margarine

1½ kg chicken,
  cut into 8 pieces,
  plus 2 extra thighs

1 onion, chopped

2 well-rounded tbsp
  plain flour

500 ml red wine

300 ml beef stock

1 bouquet garni

1 beef stock cube

1 heaped tsp tomato paste

3 shallots, finely chopped

1 clove garlic,
  finely chopped

For the garnish

12–15 pickling onions
  (or whole shallots)

a little butter

60 g continental bacon
  (speck), cut into bite-
  sized pieces (lardons)

150 g champignons
  (button mushrooms)

1 tsp sugar

2 tbsp chopped parsley

DF

METHOD

In a large casserole or a deep frying pan with a lid, heat the margarine and fry the chicken pieces until well browned. (Use margarine because butter burns, and oil sits unabsorbed on the top of the sauce.) Add the onion and allow to brown a little also. Sprinkle the flour over, and stir to the bottom of the pan to form a roux (you may need a little extra margarine if the pan is too dry to absorb the flour). Add the liquids, bouquet garni, stock cube, tomato paste, shallots and garlic, and season with salt and freshly milled black pepper. Place the lid on and simmer gently for about 45 minutes, turning the chicken pieces once.

Meanwhile, boil the onions for the garnish in salted water until softened (the time depends on their size), then drain and set aside. When the chicken is cooked, heat some butter in a small frying pan and fry the bacon until crisp and rendered. Add to the chicken. In the rendered bacon fat, plus more butter if necessary, fry the champignons – whole if tiny, or cut into chunky pieces. When fried, add to the casserole. Fry the cooked small onions, adding the sugar to caramelise them a little, then add to the chicken.

To serve, transfer the chicken pieces to a serving platter. Boil down the sauce to a nice sauce consistency. Check the seasoning, and coat the chicken with the sauce and garnish. Sprinkle with the parsley.

NICK HONEYMAN
PARIS BUTTER & LE PETIT LÉON

For me, lasagne was my go-to dish as a child and my favourite time of the week was when my mother would crack one out. This recipe is my fun, modern interpretation of a Kiwiana classic, using fresh beetroot as a replacement for pasta, and snapper instead of meat sauce. These days, I prefer something a little bit lighter and fresher in an age where people are a little more conscious about what we are putting into our bodies each day. Having a good diet is pretty helpful to battle the stresses of the day – so, if I can make food a bit healthier, I'm hopefully doing everyone a favour!

Nick

Herne Bay,
Auckland

SHAVED VEGETABLES

Recipes by NICK HONEYMAN, Paris Butter & Le Petit Léon, Auckland, New Zealand

SERVINGS: 4 | PREP TIME: 15 MINS PLUS CHILLING | COOK TIME: 1 MIN | SKILL LEVEL: 1 (EASY)

INGREDIENTS

500 g any seasonal baby
  vegetables (e.g. radish,
  beetroot, carrot, turnip,
  fennel)
1 litre water
30 g salt
100 ml olive oil

DF, GF, V

METHOD

Cut each vegetable in half lengthways. Using a Japanese mandolin, slice each vegetable on its cut side to 2 mm thick. Place slices in a bowl of ice water for 1 hour.

Bring water, salt and olive oil to the boil. Strain the vegetables and blanch them in the olive oil water for 1 minute, until al dente. Strain, and serve immediately.

BEETROOT & SNAPPER LASAGNE

SERVINGS: 4 | PREP TIME: 45 MINS | COOK TIME: 4–6 MINS | SKILL LEVEL: 2 (MODERATE)

INGREDIENTS

2 large fresh beetroots
  (red or yellow)
4 pickling onions
1 clove garlic
1 snapper fillet, skinned
  (or any white-fleshed
  fish, around 300 g
  approx.)
30 g butter
2 tbsp olive oil
zest of 1 lemon
20 g chopped fresh
  parsley
200 g brie
50 g Parmesan,
  finely grated
a couple of handfuls
  of freshly picked greens

GF

METHOD

Wash beetroot, place in a deep pot and cover with water. Add a tablespoon of sea salt and bring to the boil. Reduce the heat and simmer until cooked, around 35 minutes. Strain beetroot and peel the skin off straight away by rubbing them with a piece of paper towel. Using a mandolin or sharp knife, cut beetroot into thin ribbons around 2 mm thick. Irregular shapes are fine: it's the thickness that is important. Lay them on a tray, reserve and keep warm until needed.

Peel onions and shave on a mandolin or finely with a knife, making sure to cut them across the grain to give perfect ringlets. Finely chop garlic and cut snapper into fine dice (1 cm). Pre-heat the oven to 180°C.

Place butter, oil and onions in a heavy-based saucepan. Gently heat the pan over a medium heat, seasoning the mixture with salt at the beginning to draw the moisture out of the onions. They will cook in 4–6 minutes over a medium heat; you do not want any colour but do want them to be translucent.

Strain onions out of the pot, reserve and keep warm, returning the cooking liquid to the pot. Add garlic. Cook gently over a low heat until garlic takes on a light caramel colour, then add snapper and remove the pan from the heat. The snapper will cook in the residual heat of the pan – it will be ready as soon as it takes on a white colour. Season with lemon zest, chopped parsley and sea salt.

To plate, cut brie into four pieces, placing one in the centre of each plate and pushing it down with the back of a spoon until about 2 cm high. Place serving plates in the oven for 3 minutes, then remove and cover brie with beetroot slices, then a layer of onion and a layer of snapper and a few greens. Repeat this one more time, then finish with beetroot slices on top. Season with olive oil and a little lemon zest, and finish the plate with a good amount of Parmesan.

TIP

Take time in the cutting of all of the ingredients – this is a very important part of the cooking process and is often where people let themselves down.

ANGIE & DAN HONG
CHEFS & RESTAURATEURS

Going to my mum's house for Monday
Hong Dinners is the highlight of my week.
I rarely say yes to going out with mates for
dinner that night because I know that no
meal will ever be as good as the one
I share with my family at that table.

DAN HONG

Newtown,
New South Wales

CHẢ GIÒ

VIETNAMESE SPRING ROLLS

Recipe by *ANGIE & DAN HONG*, chefs & restaurateurs, New South Wales, Australia

MAKES: 60 | **PREP TIME: 30 MINS** | **COOK TIME: 20–30 MINS** | **SKILL LEVEL: 2 (MODERATE)**

INGREDIENTS

For the filling

500 g minced pork neck

½ cup water chestnuts, finely chopped

½ cup of each of the following, all shredded:

wood ear mushrooms

shiitake mushrooms

carrot

onion

mung bean thread (1 cm lengths, softened in cold water)

Seasoning

2 tsp table salt

4 tsp raw sugar

1 tsp ground white pepper

To finish

1 tbsp dark soy sauce

1 packet medium-sized rice paper wrappers

vegetable oil, for deep-frying

DF

METHOD

In a mixing bowl, combine the filling ingredients with the seasonings and mix thoroughly.

Carefully pour hot water into a shallow, wide dish along with the soy sauce. Stir to combine. Take a rice paper wrapper and quickly immerse it in the hot water, then place on a clean, dry plate. Spoon a tablespoon of the mixture into the centre of the rice paper in a sausage shape. Fold the top and bottom ends in, then roll the rice paper up like a cigar. Set aside and repeat until all of the mixture has been used up.

Heat the oil in a heavy-based pot until it reaches 180°C. In small batches, fry the spring rolls for 7–10 minutes or until the outside is crisp and golden. Drain onto paper towel and serve hot with your favourite dipping sauce.

CHINESE ROASTED PORK BELLY
WITH QUICK-PICKLED CUCUMBER

Recipe by *ANTHONY HOY FONG*, chef & TV presenter, Auckland, New Zealand

SERVINGS: 6 | PREP TIME: 15 MINS PLUS MARINATING | COOK TIME: 2 HOURS | SKILL LEVEL: 2 (MODERATE)

INGREDIENTS

For the pork belly

1½ kg boneless slab of
  pork belly, skin on
1 tsp mānuka honey
1 tsp sugar
3 cloves garlic, crushed
3 tbsp hoisin sauce
1 tbsp soy sauce
1 tbsp sea salt, plus extra
  for rubbing
½ tsp five-spice powder
1 tbsp canola oil
fresh coriander leaves,
  to garnish
spring onions, to garnish

For the pickled cucumber

1 large cucumber
2½ tbsp seasoned rice
  vinegar
2 tbsp water
1 tbsp sugar
1 tbsp toasted sesame oil
1 tsp sea salt
1 medium-sized fresh red
  chilli, finely sliced

DF

METHOD

Place pork skin-side down on board and slice three-quarters deep into the flesh at 4 cm intervals (this will allow the marinade to get deep into the meat). Place pork on roasting rack in a clean sink and pour boiling-hot water over both sides 2–3 times to tighten skin (this helps the crackling process). Pat dry with paper towels and place in foil-lined roasting pan.

Make marinade by combining honey, sugar, garlic, hoisin, soy, 1 tablespoon salt and five-spice powder. Rub marinade all over flesh of pork, getting it deep into the slices but avoiding the skin – if you get any on the skin, wipe it off with a paper towel as it will prevent the skin from crackling.

With pork skin-side up in pan, use the tip of a sharp knife to dock the skin all over with small slashes. Rub skin with canola oil and a little salt. Place in fridge to marinate for 2–3 hours.

Pre-heat the oven to 240°C. Place pork in centre of oven and cook for 20 minutes. Add 2 cups of water to pan, then reduce heat to 160°C and cook for 1½ hours. Finish under grill for 3–4 minutes to crackle skin further if required (use foil to cover any edges that get too brown). Remove from oven and rest for 15 minutes before slicing.

Peel cucumber, then slice lengthwise in half. Using a small spoon, scrape out seeds and discard. Slice halves lengthwise into thirds, then cut into small wedges (approximately 2 cm). In a medium-sized bowl, place vinegar, water, sugar, sesame oil, salt and chilli. Whisk together, then add cucumber. Cover with plastic wrap and place in fridge for 30 minutes before serving.

Cut pork into strips using the original deep cuts as a guide. Slice each strip into bite-sized pieces and arrange on platters. Serve with pickled cucumber. Garnish with coriander and sliced spring onions.

DAN HUNTER
BRAE

I love the ease and simplicity of roasting a chicken with a few vegetables and herbs in season. It's a dish my dad used to cook a lot when I was growing up. It really is just a matter of 'throw together in one pan, open a bottle of wine and wait'.

–Dan

Birregurra, Victoria

SUMMER ROAST CHICKEN

Recipe by *DAN HUNTER*, Brae, Victoria, Australia

SERVINGS: 4 – OR 2 HUNGRY ADULTS & A 4-YEAR-OLD | PREP TIME: 20 MINS | COOK TIME: 45 MINS
SKILL LEVEL: 1 (EASY)

INGREDIENTS

For the chicken

1 x 1½ kg organic chicken

a handful of tarragon,
  thyme, fennel tops,
  lovage (mixed)

1 lemon, cut in half

1 head garlic, cut in half

olive oil to coat

generous amount of good
  quality salt

For the vegetables

2–4 small zucchini,
  with flowers intact

2–6 small tomatoes
  per person

as many potatoes as
  you feel like (such as
  Bintje, Kipfler or
  small Dutch Creams)

a handful of chopped
  chives

DF, GF

METHOD

For the chicken: take the chicken from the fridge and out of any plastic packaging about 20–30 minutes before you want to cook it. Pre-heat the oven to 220°C.

Dislocate the chicken legs at the thigh muscle, laying the legs flat but still attached, and remove the wishbone. (This shortens the usual cooking time.)

Stuff herbs, lemon halves and garlic into the cavity and smother the skin with olive oil. Sprinkle a good amount of salt over the skin, and rub the oil and salt into it. Place the chicken on a roasting tray.

For the veg: harvest the veg fresh if possible – all are best just picked. Wash the veg and cut them simply, leaving some of the zucchini flowers whole and splitting the larger ones. Quarter the bigger tomatoes and leave the small ones whole. Peel and cut the potatoes into quarters, or lengthways if using Kipflers.

Arrange the zucchini and tomato around the chicken. Dress everything well with olive oil, season with salt, and place the tray on the bottom rack of the oven.

With the potatoes, it's best to roast them separately and unseasoned so that they crisp up well. Place them in a separate baking dish, cover well with olive oil and place the tray on the top shelf of the oven.

If all goes to plan, everything will be ready in 45 minutes. I leave the oven at 220°C the whole time, then open the door with the oven turned off for 10 minutes once everything is cooked so that the juices distribute nicely through the chicken. Season the zucchini and tomatoes with chives, season the potatoes to taste, carve the chook and serve.

BURNT GARLIC, CHILLI & LEMON SQUID

Recipe by *NADIYA HUSSAIN*, baker, cook & food writer, Leeds, England

SERVINGS: 5 | **PREP TIME: 30 MINS** | **COOK TIME: 5 MINS** | **SKILL LEVEL: 1 (EASY)**

INGREDIENTS

4 whole squid with
  tentacles (or 25 baby
  squid), cleaned

4 cloves garlic

3 tbsp olive oil

1 lemon, sliced into 8 slices

2 tbsp chopped coriander

2 spring onions, finely
  chopped

1 whole red chilli, finely
  chopped

½ tsp pink peppercorns,
  crushed

oil, for cooking

DF, GF

METHOD

Cut the squid into pieces of roughly similar size, and score with a knife, making sure not to cut all the way through the flesh.

Place the garlic cloves in a heatproof bowl, or a metal bowl. Blow-torch the pieces of garlic with the skins on till they are completely black. Chop the burnt garlic into small pieces, making sure not to discard any of the charred black bits; all this adds to the flavour (you can also cook them under a very hot grill).

To the garlic add the lemon slices, squeezing some juice out of each slice. Then add the coriander, spring onions, red chilli, salt to taste and pink peppercorns. Give it all a good stir.

Place a frying pan on a medium heat and add oil, and when the oil is hot add the squid. Give it a good stir and after a few seconds add the spicy mix in. Cook for about 4 minutes. You know it's done when it curls up and looks less translucent.

Do not overcook, or the squid will become rubbery.

PHILIP JOHNSON
E'CCO BISTRO

This dish reminds me of my time in London as a young chef with friends. We made a caramel, threw in brandy, rum, some bananas, then popped some pastry on top. When it was done we turned it onto a board, topped it with ice cream and ate it straight from the board. Great times!

Brisbane,
Queensland

BANANA TARTE TATIN
WITH RUM & RAISIN ICE CREAM

Recipe by *PHILIP JOHNSON*, E'cco Bistro, Queensland, Australia

SERVINGS: 6 | PREP TIME: 40 MINS PLUS SOAKING OVERNIGHT & CHILLING/CHURNING
COOK TIME: 10–12 MINS | SKILL LEVEL: 2 (MODERATE)

INGREDIENTS

For the ice cream
150 g raisins
125 ml (½ cup) dark rum
300 g caster sugar
12 egg yolks
500 ml (2 cups) milk
500 ml (2 cups) cream

For the tarte tatin
1 roll frozen butter
  puff pastry, defrosted
  (or use thinly rolled
  homemade pastry)
6 large bananas
250 g caster sugar
60 ml (¼ cup) water
80 ml (⅓ cup) dark rum
60 ml (¼ cup) cream
1 egg, beaten,
  for egg wash

V

METHOD

For the ice cream: soak raisins in dark rum overnight.

In a large bowl, whisk together sugar and egg yolks. Place milk and cream in a 2-litre saucepan and bring almost to the boil. Whisk hot milk mixture into the egg mix, then return to a clean saucepan and place over a moderate heat. Using a wooden spoon, stir constantly until custard thickens and coats the back of the spoon. Do not let mixture boil. Strain through a fine sieve, then refrigerate until cold.

Churn cold ice cream mixture in an ice cream machine. Once fully churned, stir rum and raisins through, and store in the freezer.

For the tarte tatin: pre-heat the oven to 220°C. Butter a 26–28 cm fry pan. Cut the puff pastry to fit the top of the pan and set aside. Peel bananas and slice thickly on the diagonal.

Combine sugar and water in a small saucepan and stir over a low heat until sugar dissolves. Bring to the boil, and boil without stirring until syrup turns to a dark caramel colour. Immediately remove from the heat and, very carefully, as caramel spits, stir in the rum. Return to a low heat and stir until smooth, then add cream and bring to the boil.

Pour the caramel into the base of the pan. Arrange sliced banana in concentric circles, then top with the puff pastry circle. Egg-wash pastry by brushing with beaten egg. Take care not to let egg run down the edge of the pastry. Bake for 10–12 minutes or until pastry is golden.

To serve: remove the tart from oven and, while still quite hot, invert tart onto the centre of a serving plate. Top each serving with a spoonful of rum and raisin ice cream.

FARRO WITH ROASTED LEEKS & SMOKY-SWEET ROMESCO

Recipe by *ANNA JONES*, cook, stylist & food writer, London, England

SERVINGS: 4–6 (WITH LEFTOVER ROMESCO) | **PREP TIME: 10 MINS** | **COOK TIME: 55 MINS**
SKILL LEVEL: 1 (EASY)

If I had my way, this smoky tangy-sweet Catalan sauce would find its way into a meal a day. The recipe will make enough for this dinner plus an extra jam-jar-full to keep in the fridge for a week or so. Farro is one of my favourite grains — it has a chewy, almost gummy texture that is so pleasing. Farro is much lower in gluten than most grains, so if you have a mild sensitivity to gluten it might be okay for you. It's available in most wholefood shops and good supermarkets. If you can't get your hands on farro, then pearl barley or bulgur wheat would also work, as would quinoa if you prefer it. Just adjust the cooking times accordingly. Use the best jarred Spanish capsicum you can find — piquillo are the ones to look out for. If you can't find baby leeks, normal leeks are fine too. Just wash, trim, halve them lengthways and cut them into 3 cm lengths.

INGREDIENTS

1 butternut squash, de-seeded and cut into rough chunks

12 whole baby leeks, washed

1 unwaxed lemon

200 g farro (or another grain)

a few sprigs of fresh parsley, leaves picked

For the romesco

100 g blanched almonds

50 g hazelnuts

olive oil, for frying

2 slices stale good white bread (about 40 g), torn into chunks

2 cloves garlic, peeled and finely chopped

1 tsp sweet smoked paprika

1 × 220 g jar roasted red capsicum, drained

6 tbsp extra virgin olive oil

2 tbsp sherry vinegar

1 small dried chilli, crumbled, or a pinch of dried chilli flakes

a generous pinch of saffron strands

1 tbsp tomato paste

DF, V

METHOD

Pre-heat the oven to 200°C/180°C fan. First make your romesco sauce. Scatter the nuts on a baking tray and roast in the hot oven for 10–15 minutes, until golden. While they are roasting, heat a little olive oil in a pan and fry the bread until golden-brown all over. Add the garlic and smoked paprika and cook for a further minute, then remove from the heat.

Leaving the oven on, transfer the nuts and toasted bread to a food processor. Add the peppers and blitz until you have a coarse paste — you still want a nice bit of texture. Tip the whole lot into a mixing bowl, stir in the extra virgin olive oil, sherry vinegar, crumbled chilli, saffron and tomato purée. Season to taste and mix well, adjusting the favours if need be. Romesco is about a balance of punchy flavours. Too thick? Add a little water. Too sweet? Add a little vinegar. Too sharp? Add a little oil to soften. Leave to one side to mellow.

Next, put the squash on a large roasting tray with the leeks. Drizzle over some olive oil, grate over the zest of the lemon and season. Roast in the oven for 40 minutes until the squash is golden and the leeks are sweet. Meanwhile, cook the farro in salted boiling water for 35–40 minutes, until it is soft but still has a good gummy bite.

Drain the farro, toss with the roasted squash and leeks and a good few tablespoons of the romesco, and finish off with a good sprinkling of parsley.

TIP

Ways to use romesco:
· spread on toast and topped with a slick of goat's cheese for a quick snack
· as a dip for baby carrots and spring veg
· as a marinade for barbecued veg
· piled onto roasted veg for extra flavour
· tossed through cooked noodles with pan-fried greens
· stirred into a bowl of brown rice and topped with a poached egg
· next to your morning eggs
· with flatbread and feta for a quick, simple lunch
· spooned on top of a bowl of soup.

Whakatane,
Bay of Plenty

JULIANS BERRY FARM

As soon as we open our doors every October, people start piling in to get their first taste of summer. The berry season is a short, intense season so we need lots of extra hands on deck. We have a lot of university and high-school students and backpackers working here. When they first turn up I like to show them another worker's hands, covered in berry juice and scratches from the berry vines. The contrast with their clean hands makes me laugh. One of my favourite parts of my job is the pastoral element that goes with it. I am interested in their futures and hope Julians Berry Farm and Café can make a positive contribution to their lives.

Paul

BERRY JAM

Recipes by *JULIANS BERRY FARM*, Bay of Plenty, New Zealand

MAKES: 7 X 300 ML JARS | COOK TIME: 40 MINS | SKILL LEVEL: 1 (EASY)

INGREDIENTS

1½ kg fresh or
   frozen raspberries,
   boysenberries, Ranui
   berries, loganberries,
   tayberries or
   blackberries
1½ kg sugar

DF, GF

METHOD

Place a couple of small plates in the fridge to chill. Wash seven 300 ml jars, rinse and place in a warm oven (100°C) to sterilise while you are making the jam, or for about 20 minutes. Sterilise lids by placing in a bowl and covering with boiling water. After a few minutes, tip into a colander and shake off all the water.

Bring berries to the boil in a large preserving pan or saucepan. Then add sugar and bring to a rapid boil. Boil rapidly for about 15 minutes. KEEP WATCHING.

Check that it's setting by placing a small amount of jam on a cold plate and returning it to the fridge for 2 minutes. Take it out and tip the plate on its side. If jam is ready, a wrinkling or skin will form on its surface. Keep testing until this happens, then bottle into sterilised jars and seal with lids while still hot.

BERRY COULIS

MAKES: ABOUT 1¼ LITRES (APPROX.) | COOK TIME: 30 MINS | SKILL LEVEL: 1 (EASY)

INGREDIENTS

1 kg frozen berries
500 g sugar
1 small cinnamon quill
2 cm x 1 cm piece
   each of lemon and
   orange peel

DF, GF

METHOD

Place all ingredients in a large saucepan and bring to the boil. Boil for 10 minutes, remove and discard peel and cinnamon, then purée in a heatproof blender or food processor until creamy. Bring back to the boil for 5 minutes. Can be bottled while hot, but serve cooled.

Will keep for three months in the fridge, or can be frozen.

FRENCH TOAST

SERVINGS: 4 | PREP TIME: 5 MINS | COOK TIME: 8 MINS | SKILL LEVEL: 1 (EASY)

INGREDIENTS

2 eggs
140 ml cream
4 tsp sugar
a few drops vanilla essence
pinch of ground cinnamon
2 baguettes
2 bananas
a few knobs of butter
8 rashers streaky bacon
6 tbsp berry coulis
6 tbsp maple syrup
whipped cream and
   fresh berries, to serve

METHOD

In a large bowl, mix eggs, cream, 2 teaspoons sugar, vanilla and cinnamon. Slice each baguette into six pieces and soak in egg mixture for 1 minute. Pre-heat the oven to 100°C.

Slice bananas in half lengthways, then halve into shorter lengths and sprinkle with remaining sugar. In a pre-heated frying pan, fry the baguette in a little butter, then place in the warm oven while frying the bacon and bananas. Bananas should be just caramelised so they still hold their shape.

To serve, dress plates with a swirl each of berry coulis and maple syrup. Build layers from three slices of baguette, two rashers of bacon and two slices of banana per serve. Drizzle with maple syrup and berry coulis, add a dollop of freshly whipped cream and garnish with fresh berries.

KYLIE KWONG
CHEF, RESTAURATEUR & TV PRESENTER

These days, a wok is as common in an Australian home
as a barbecue and a frying pan. And I just love stir-frying
because of the way the high heat cooks food so quickly
and beautifully with all their caramelly flavours and so on.
It's so accessible and simple.

Potts Point,
New South Wales

STIR-FRIED HOKKIEN NOODLES WITH CHICKEN, CHILLI & BEAN SPROUTS

Recipe by *KYLIE KWONG*, chef, restaurateur & TV presenter, New South Wales, Australia

SERVINGS: 4 | **PREP TIME: 30 MINS** | **COOK TIME: 8 MINS** | **SKILL LEVEL: 1 (EASY)**

INGREDIENTS

400 g chicken thigh fillets,
  cut into 2 cm slices

¼ cup vegetable oil

1 small white onion,
  cut in half and then
  into thick wedges

12 slices fresh ginger

1 x 450 g packet fresh
  Hokkien noodles

2 tbsp Shaoxing wine
  or dry sherry

1 tbsp white sugar

2 tbsp light soy sauce

1 tbsp malt vinegar

½ tsp sesame oil

1 cup fresh bean sprouts

½ cup julienned
  spring onion

2 large red chillies, finely
  sliced on the diagonal

For the marinade

1 tbsp white sugar

1 tbsp light soy sauce

1 tbsp Shaoxing wine
  or dry sherry

½ tsp sesame oil

DF

METHOD

Combine the chicken with marinade ingredients in a bowl, cover, and leave to marinate in the fridge for 30 minutes.

Heat 2 tablespoons of the oil in a hot wok until the surface seems to shimmer slightly. Add chicken and stir-fry for 1 minute. Remove from wok and set aside.

Add remaining oil to hot wok with onion and ginger, and stir-fry for 1 minute or until onion is lightly browned. Toss in noodles, reserved chicken, wine or sherry, sugar, soy sauce, vinegar and sesame oil, and stir-fry for 1½ minutes. Add bean sprouts, spring onion and half the chilli, and stir-fry for a further 30 seconds or until chicken is just cooked through and the noodles are hot.

Arrange noodles in bowls, top with remaining chilli and serve immediately.

NIGELLA LAWSON
FOOD WRITER & TV BROADCASTER

This cake is magnificent in its damp blackness.
I can't say that you can absolutely taste the stout
in it, but there is certainly a resonant, ferrous tang,
which I happen to love. The best way of describing
it is to say that it's like gingerbread without
the spices. There is enough sugar – a certain
understatement here – to counter any potential
bitterness of the Guinness, and although I've eaten
versions of this made up like a chocolate sandwich
cake, stuffed and slathered in a rich chocolate icing,
I think that can take away from its dark majesty.

Besides, I wanted to make a cream-cheese frosting
to echo the pale head that sits on top of a glass
of stout. It's unconventional to add cream, but
it makes it frothier and lighter, which I regard as
aesthetically and gastronomically desirable. But it
is perfectly acceptable to leave the cake un-iced;
in fact, it tastes gorgeous plain.

NIGELLA

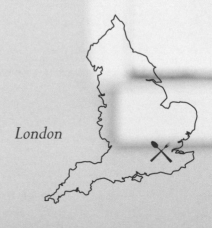

London

CHOCOLATE GUINNESS CAKE

Recipe by *NIGELLA LAWSON*, food writer & TV broadcaster, London, England

SERVINGS: 12 | **PREP TIME: 15 MINS** | **COOK TIME: 1 HOUR** | **SKILL LEVEL: 1 (EASY)**

INGREDIENTS

For the cake
250 ml Guinness
250 g unsalted butter
75 g cocoa
400 g caster sugar
1 x 150 ml pot sour cream
2 eggs
1 tbsp real vanilla extract
275 g plain flour
2½ tsp bicarbonate of
  soda

For the topping
300 g cream cheese
  (I use Philadelphia)
150 g icing sugar
125 ml double or
  whipping cream

V

METHOD

Pre-heat the oven to 180°C, and butter and line a 23 cm springform tin.

Pour the Guinness into a large, wide saucepan, add the butter – in spoons or slices – and heat until the butter's melted, at which time you should whisk in the cocoa and sugar. Beat the sour cream with the eggs and vanilla and then pour into the brown, buttery, beery pan and finally whisk in the flour and bicarb.

Pour the cake batter into the greased and lined tin and bake for 45 minutes to an hour. Leave to cool completely in the tin on a cooling rack, as it is quite a damp cake.

When the cake's cold, sit it on a flat platter or cake stand and get on with the icing. Lightly whip the cream cheese until smooth, sieve over the icing sugar and then beat them both together. Or do this in a processor, putting the unsieved icing sugar in first and blitzing to remove lumps before adding the cheese.

Add the cream and beat again until it makes a spreadable consistency. Ice the top of the black cake so that it resembles the frothy top of the famous pint.

JULIE LE CLERC
CHEF & FOOD WRITER

This recipe is very close to my heart, as it represents my mother's Syrian heritage. It wasn't until a few years ago – in an attempt to piece together my own history – that I connected with my Syrian extended family for the very first time. When I arrived in Damascus, my great aunts Nabiha and Hind were so overjoyed I had reunited the families that they rallied together for days to cook and celebrate! Now when I cook this recipe at home, I am taken back to all those feelings of generosity, warmth, flavours and family. I believe, no matter where you are from, feeding people really is the most wonderful way to show love.

Julie

Westmere,
Auckland

SYRIAN FATTOUSH SALAD

Recipe by *JULIE LE CLERC*, chef & food writer, Auckland, New Zealand

SERVINGS: 4 | **PREP TIME: 10 MINS** | **COOK TIME: 10–15 MINS** | **SKILL LEVEL: 1 (EASY)**

INGREDIENTS

2 large rounds stale pita bread

olive oil

2 small Lebanese cucumbers

8 medium-sized ripe tomatoes

1 small red onion

4–5 radishes

⅓ cup chopped fresh parsley

⅓ cup chopped fresh coriander

3 tbsp chopped fresh mint

1 tbsp sumac (optional)

For the lemon dressing

1 clove garlic, finely crushed

juice of 1 lemon

3–4 tbsp pomegranate molasses

⅓ cup extra virgin olive oil

DF, GF, V

METHOD

Break bread into bite-sized pieces, drizzle with a little oil and toss well to coat. Bake for 10–15 minutes in an oven pre-heated to 180°C, tossing once or twice, until golden. Alternatively, toast in a large frying pan, turning often until crisp and golden. Remove to cool.

Dice cucumbers, tomatoes and onion and thinly slice radishes. Combine in a bowl with herbs and season well with salt and freshly ground black pepper.

Blend dressing ingredients together. The dressing needs to taste fairly sharp and lemony – adjust with extra lemon juice if necessary. Pour dressing over salad ingredients and toss well to coat.

Finally, toss pita pieces through (don't dress too far in advance, or the bread will turn soggy). Sprinkle with sumac, if available.

TIPS

Sumac is a sour-tasting, ground, red-berry spice, available in specialist food stores and some supermarkets. Don't worry if you can't find it: the salad will still be delicious.

If pomegranate molasses isn't available, then substitute with more lemon juice.

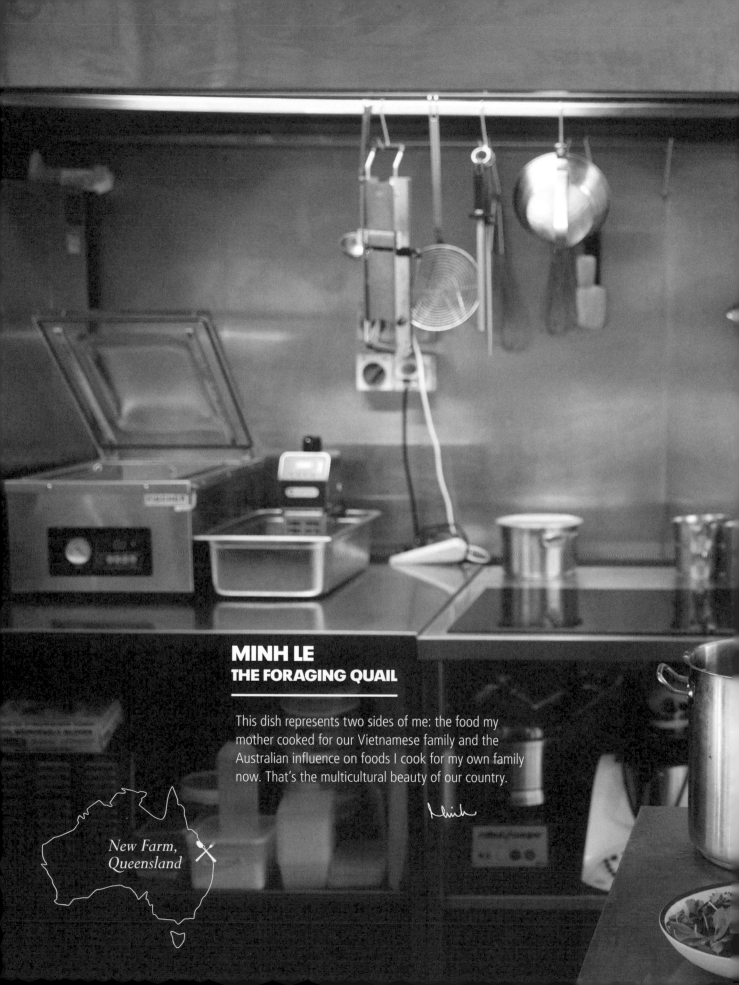

MINH LE
THE FORAGING QUAIL

This dish represents two sides of me: the food my
mother cooked for our Vietnamese family and the
Australian influence on foods I cook for my own family
now. That's the multicultural beauty of our country.

*New Farm,
Queensland*

SPICY VIETNAMESE CHICKEN WINGS

Recipe by MINH LÊ, The Foraging Quail, Queensland, Australia

SERVINGS: 6 | PREP TIME: 25 MINS PLUS MARINATING OVERNIGHT | COOK TIME: 2–3 HOURS
SKILL LEVEL: 2 (MODERATE)

INGREDIENTS

100 g fresh ginger
5 bird's eye chillies
100 g garlic, peeled
20 g ground black pepper
1 kg chicken wings
50 ml olive oil
1 kg caster sugar
200 ml fish sauce
6 eggs
1 bunch coriander
1 bunch Thai basil
1 bunch Vietnamese mint
1 bunch mint
2 cups jasmine rice

DF, GF

METHOD

Peel ginger and chop into 1 cm pieces. Place ginger, chillies, garlic and pepper in a food processor and blend to a paste. Cut chicken wings into three, along the joints of the bone, and place in a bowl with the paste. Stir to coat the chicken with the paste, and marinate overnight.

Pour olive oil into a deep saucepan along with sugar. Over a high heat, keep stirring until the sugar is starting to brown and caramelise, then quickly add the marinated chicken wings to the pan. Let the caramel coat the chicken wings – you must keep stirring the whole time.

Once chicken is fully coated, deglaze with fish sauce. Turn heat down to low, put a lid on the pan and let it simmer for 2–3 hours. Make sure to stir every 15 minutes.

In another saucepan, boil eggs for 3 minutes, then refresh in ice water. Peel eggs and add them to the chicken wings 30 minutes before the wings finish.

Pick off all the herb leaves and wash. Set aside to eat fresh with the rice. Wash rice three times, place in a rice cooker (or saucepan), add 2 cups of water and cook until done (about 25 minutes in a rice cooker or 20 minutes on the stovetop; I highly recommend using a rice cooker).

GARY LEE
THE IVY

I like to share – everyone should be able to get a little bit of what everybody else is having. This dish is like that – there's a leg of lamb, sliced and roasted, and a big bowl of tabbouleh which everyone can dip into and help themselves. One of the reasons we serve it at The Ivy is because London is very multicultural. People from all walks of life come into the restaurant, and part of its appeal is that it's Middle Eastern-style food – very light and very, very healthy!

Covent Garden, London

THE IVY'S MOROCCAN SPICED RUMP OF LAMB WITH HUMMUS, HARISSA & SMOKED EGGPLANT

Recipe by *GARY LEE*, The Ivy, London, England

SERVINGS: 2 | **PREP TIME: 40 MINS PLUS SOAKING** | **COOK TIME: 1 HOUR 45 MINS**
SKILL LEVEL: 2 (MODERATE)

INGREDIENTS

2 rumps of lamb, approximately 200 g each (approx.), fully trimmed

2 tsp harissa

For the hummus

100 g raw chickpeas, soaked overnight in cold water

2 cloves garlic, crushed with 1 tsp salt

juice of 1 lemon

60 ml (4 tbsp) tahini paste, stirred well

For the dukkah

8 tbsp sesame seeds

4 tbsp coriander seeds

2 tbsp cumin seeds

40 g hazelnuts

1 tsp salt

½ tsp freshly ground pepper

For the smoked eggplant (baba ghanoush)

800 g eggplant

1 clove garlic, peeled and crushed

¾ tsp salt

2½ tbsp light tahini or ½ tbsp sesame oil

3–4 tbsp lemon juice

¼ tsp cayenne pepper

1–2 tbsp extra virgin olive oil

DF, GF

METHOD

To make the hummus, take the chickpeas that have been soaking overnight, and while they are still in water, and rub them with your fingers to loosen their skins. These will float to the surface and can then be discarded. Place the chickpeas in fresh water and cook for 40–60 minutes on the hob until they are tender. Strain them, being careful to retain the cooking liquid. Place the drained chickpeas in a food processor with the crushed garlic, lemon juice, tahini and 2 tablespoons of the cooking liquid. Blend until the mixture is smooth, adding more cooking liquid if required, and season with salt and pepper. Leave to one side.

To make the dukkah, roast all the ingredients, except for the salt and pepper, separately on a baking sheet. If the hazelnuts have skins on them, these can be removed after roasting by rubbing the nuts in a cloth. Pound the roasted seeds in a mortar and pestle or gently blend them in a food processor, being careful not to over-blend them so that they form an oily paste. Combine the seeds, nuts and salt and pepper, and keep in an airtight container until ready to use.

To make the smoked eggplant, pre-heat the grill. Slit the skin of each eggplant once or twice. Place them on a baking sheet and place under the pre-heated grill 10 cm from the element. Grill for 20–30 minutes or until the skin is blackened, blistered and burnt, and the pulp is soft. Turn them once. Remove from the grill and allow to cool slightly. Scrape the pulp from the skin and place it in a blender. Purée for a few seconds and then add the garlic, salt, tahini or sesame oil, lemon juice, cayenne pepper and olive oil. Blend well.

Pre-heat the oven to 200°C/180°C fan. Season the rumps of lamb and seal in a pre-heated frying pan for at least 4–5 minutes to ensure that all the flavours are locked in, and then place in the hot oven for 3–4 minutes. Once cooked, remove the lamb from the oven and allow it to rest for 5 minutes, loosely covered in foil, saving the cooking sauces to one side.

When ready to serve, place a small amount of harissa onto each plate and a large spoonful of hummus adjacent to it; finish with a drizzle of olive oil. Slice the warm lamb rumps and arrange on the plates. Sprinkle the lamb with the dukkah and finish with a little jus from the meat. Serve with the smoked eggplant.

NORMANDY TART MADE WITH A FOOD PROCESSOR

Recipe by *PRUE LEITH OBE, CBE*, restaurateur, caterer & food writer, Gloucestershire, England

SERVINGS: 8–10 | **PREP TIME: 45 MINS PLUS CHILLING** | **COOK TIME: 45 MINS** | **SKILL LEVEL: 2 (MODERATE)**

INGREDIENTS

For the pastry
225 g plain flour
140 g butter
1 egg
pinch of salt
50 g caster sugar

For the almond filling
170 g butter
170 g caster sugar
225 g ground almonds
2 eggs
1 tbsp calvados, kirsch,
  or whatever liqueur
  you like
a few drops almond
  essence

For the topping
3–5 eating apples,
  depending on size
half a 340 g jar of smooth
  apricot jam, warmed
  with 1 tbsp water to
  a thick syrup

V

METHOD

Set the oven at 200°C and put a metal tray in it to heat.

Whizz everything for the pastry together until the mixture forms a ball. Roll out between two sheets of polythene until big enough to line a 25 cm flan ring. Chill for 30 minutes. If the dish is porcelain, bake blind; if metal, don't bother. To bake blind, line the pastry-lined flan ring with baking parchment and fill with baking beans. Bake for 10 minutes, then remove the beans and paper and bake for a further 5–10 minutes or until the pastry is light golden all over.

Whizz everything for the filling in the food processor (no need to wash the bowl after making the pastry), then spread in the flan case.

Peel the apples if you like, but no need to. Core them and cut in half from top to stalk end. Slice each half-apple finely, keeping the slices in order. Arrange them on top of the filling.

Set the flan in the middle of the hot oven and bake for 15 minutes. Then paint with hot jam. Reduce the oven temperature to 180°C and bake for half an hour or so, until the filling is firm and brown. Remove from the oven and give it another brush with the jam if you think it needs it.

To serve: best cooled to tepid or room temperature without refrigeration. If you make it in advance, freeze it and then reheat for 20 minutes at 180°C and allow to cool. This will crisp up the pastry again.

VICTOR & EVELYN LIONG
LEE HO FOOK

We don't really have that many days off together, but when we do, it generally involves eating. We'll go out to eat dumplings, noodles, spicy Sichuan food and there's always a drink or two involved. Working together as siblings can get a little tough, but it's nice to take a few minutes to debrief and then we don't talk about work – we're siblings again.

Victor + Ev

*Collingwood,
Victoria*

SWEET & SOUR PORK

Recipes by *VICTOR & EVELYN LIONG*, Lee Ho Fook, Victoria, Australia

**SERVINGS: 4 | PREP TIME: 3½ HOURS PLUS MARINATING | COOK TIME: 20 MINS PLUS SAUCE-MAKING
SKILL LEVEL: 1 (EASY)**

INGREDIENTS

For the sweet and sour sauce
100 g onions, sliced
20 g long red chillies, sliced
40 g cloves garlic, smashed
80 ml vegetable oil, for cooking
125 g strawberries, sliced
500 ml chicken stock
120 ml white vinegar
25 ml Japanese soy sauce
130 g sugar
40 ml Shaoxing rice wine
120 ml Heinz Big Red Tomato Sauce
100 g pineapple, diced

Marinade
50 ml Japanese soy sauce
50 ml Shaoxing rice wine
15 g chicken stock powder
20 g sugar
1 tsp salt
2 tsp sesame oil
⅛ tsp (1 g) five-spice powder
5 g (1 clove) garlic, microplaned

For the pork
300 g organic pork neck,
  cut into 1½ cm cubes
oil, for deep-frying

Starch mix
100 g rice flour
100 g tapioca starch

To finish
20 g long red chillies, sliced thinly
20 g spring onions, cut into batons
10 g pineapple, diced finely
10 g carrot, sliced thinly
30 g kuzu starch
  (available in any Japanese
  or specialist Asian grocer)
40 ml cold water

DF

METHOD

For the sauce: stir-fry onion, chilli and garlic in the oil in a wok until caramelised, then add remaining ingredients and cook on a simmer for at least 3 hours, or until the strawberries have lost their vibrant red colour and have begun to turn white. Strain and cool.

For the pork: mix all marinade ingredients together until dissolved. Marinate the pork neck cubes in the marinade for at least 6 hours.

Place oil in a deep pan and heat to 180°C. Drain pork of excess marinade, dredge in starch mix until well coated, and deep-fry for 3–4 minutes, until pork is cooked.

To finish: stir-fry vegetables in a little oil until aromatic. Add sweet and sour sauce and bring to the boil, then thicken with a slurry of kuzu starch mixed with water. Add pork. Stir-fry until pork is coated in sauce and serve immediately.

FRIED RICE

SERVINGS: 4 | PREP TIME: 45 MINS PLUS DRYING OVERNIGHT | COOK TIME: 15 MINS | SKILL LEVEL: 1 (EASY)

INGREDIENTS
200 g jasmine rice
80 ml vegetable oil
2 eggs
1 egg yolk
1 tsp salt
1 tsp sugar
1 tsp chicken stock powder
50 g sliced spring onions
30 g butter, melted

GF

METHOD

Wash rice with cold water and drain, repeating three times more. Place drained rice in a rice cooker, add 220 g water and cook according to manufacturer's instructions. If you don't have a rice cooker, place drained rice in a pot with 220 g water. Bring to boil over a medium heat, cover and reduce heat to low. Allow to cook for 25 minutes covered, then remove from the heat and leave to stand for a further 15 minutes, still covered. Fluff grains up with a fork. Leave rice uncovered in fridge overnight to dry out.

The next day, heat vegetable oil in a wok, add eggs and yolk and scramble slightly. Before egg sets, add rice and stir-fry until grains separate. Continue stir-frying until rice is hot, then add seasonings (salt, pepper and stock powder) and stir through. Add spring onion and stir-fry until rawness has been cooked out, then drizzle butter over and serve.

CHRISTINE MANFIELD
CHEF & AUTHOR

Food should turn on your taste buds and it should never be taken too seriously! I like food that is a little irreverent, a bit whimsical, a bit pop art. All these elements play out in my head when I put dishes together. It's about seduction – you should want to just dive right in.

Christine

*Elizabeth Bay,
New South Wales*

TAMARIND PRAWNS & EGGPLANT

Recipe by *CHRISTINE MANFIELD*, chef & author, New South Wales, Australia

SERVINGS: 4 | PREP TIME: 15 MINS | COOK TIME: 10 MINS | SKILL LEVEL: 1 (EASY)

INGREDIENTS

16 cherry tomatoes
1¼ litres oil, for deep-frying
2 tbsp curry leaves
1 eggplant (300 g approx.)
400 g raw king prawn
 tail meat
1 tsp ground turmeric
1 tsp Kashmiri chilli powder
2 tsp roasted ground
 coriander
1 tsp salt
2 tbsp sunflower oil
4 tbsp chopped
 coriander leaves

For the tamarind sauce
150 g tamarind pulp
300 ml water
2 tbsp sunflower oil
1 tsp brown mustard seeds
1 tsp fenugreek seeds
6 red shallots, finely diced
12 curry leaves
2 small green chillies,
 minced
1 tbsp ginger and garlic
 paste
2 ripe tomatoes,
 de-seeded and chopped
1 tsp Kashmiri chilli powder
½ tsp ground turmeric
1 tsp roasted ground
 coriander
1 tsp sea salt flakes

DF, GF

METHOD

Pre-heat oven to 160°C. Cut tomatoes in half and roast in oven for 15 minutes. Set aside.

Heat 300 ml of the oil to 160°C in a small saucepan. Add curry leaves (they will sputter) and fry for 10 seconds. Remove with a mesh spoon and drain on a paper towel. Set aside.

Heat remaining oil to 180°C in a deep-fryer or deep saucepan. Cut eggplant into chunks and deep-fry until golden. Set aside.

De-vein and butterfly the prawn tails. Pat dry. Mix turmeric, chilli powder, ground coriander and salt with just enough water to make a paste. Stir prawns into the paste and toss to coat. Set aside while you prepare the sauce.

Tamarind sauce: break tamarind pulp into pieces and place in a small saucepan with water. Bring to the boil, remove from the heat and leave for 10 minutes, then further break up tamarind in the water with your fingers. Press through a chinois sieve to extract tamarind liquid; discard solids.

Heat oil in a frying pan over a medium heat and add mustard seeds. When they start to pop, add fenugreek seeds and fry for a few seconds, being careful not to burn them (if you burn them, they become bitter).

Add shallots, curry leaves and green chilli and cook over a moderate heat for about 2 minutes, until softened but not coloured.

Stir in ginger and garlic paste and sauté for 1 minute, then add tomato and cook for 2 minutes until softened.

Add spices, salt and tamarind liquid and bring to simmering point. Simmer the sauce until it thickens, about 5 minutes.

To cook the prawns, heat sunflower oil in a frying pan and fry prawns over a high heat for 2 minutes until just cooked and starting to colour, then add prawns to the sauce along with the roasted cherry tomatoes and fried eggplant, and stir to combine. Cook for 1 minute only, then remove from heat and stir through the chopped coriander. Scatter with fried curry leaves and serve.

STEFANO MANFREDI
CHEF, AUTHOR & RESTAURATEUR

This dish has a familiarity about it; it feels like an old friend. Spaghetti and meatballs (which is American and not Italian) belongs to the world now and everyone has a version of it. That's what keeps cuisine going. That's why you cook. Because you're trying to perfect a recipe for the people you love.

Stefano

Camperdown,
New South Wales

BUCATINI ALL'AMERICANA
SPAGHETTI & MEATBALLS

Recipe by *STEFANO MANFREDI*, chef, author & restaurateur, New South Wales, Australia

SERVINGS: 6–8 | **PREP TIME: 45–60 MINS** | **COOK TIME: 15–20 MINS** | **SKILL LEVEL: 1 (EASY)**

INGREDIENTS

*For the tomato salsa
(makes 500 ml)*

4 tbsp extra virgin olive oil

1 medium-sized onion,
  finely diced

2 cloves garlic, peeled
  and minced

1 small leek, trimmed and
  cut into fine half-rounds

1 stick celery from the
  heart, finely chopped

650 g canned Italian peeled
  tomatoes, mashed

1 tsp fennel seeds

For the meatballs

500 g lean pork shoulder

100 g pork fat

100 g mortadella (Italian
  sausage)

100 g day-old bread,
  crusts removed

⅓ cup milk

1 tsp finely chopped thyme

1 tbsp finely chopped sage

2 tbsp finely chopped parsley

2 tbsp minced garlic

1 tsp ground nutmeg

100 g grated Parmesan,
  plus extra to serve

1 egg

plain flour, for rolling

80 g bucatini per person

METHOD

Heat olive oil in a pan and gently fry onion, garlic, leek and celery until transparent. Add tomato and fennel seeds. Season with a couple of pinches of salt and some pepper. Stir well, and simmer until sauce thickens and most of the liquid has evaporated.

Mince together pork, pork fat and mortadella using a hand or an electric mincer. Soak bread in milk until milk is mostly absorbed. Add bread, minus any milk that's not absorbed, to mince mixture along with herbs, garlic, nutmeg, Parmesan and egg. Mix well with your hands, taking care to incorporate all the ingredients. Add salt and pepper to taste. A good way to taste for seasoning is to fry a small patty made from the mixture in a little olive oil; adjust if necessary.

Roll mixture into meatballs approximately 2½–3 cm in diameter, lightly flouring your hands so they don't stick. Once all the meatballs are ready, poach them in lightly simmering tomato sauce for 15–20 minutes. (Any leftover meatballs can be frozen, tightly sealed on a tray.)

Cook the bucatini to al dente according to packet instructions, and serve tossed gently with the meatballs. Sprinkle with Parmesan to taste.

TIPS

The pork fat called for is the sort that goes into making sausages and salami so succulent. Ask your butcher.

Bucatini are thick spaghetti with a hole in the middle. I think that thicker-gauge long pasta works better with the meatballs.

PETER MANIFIS
INCONTRO

It feels like food has been an important part
of my life for as long as I can remember.
While most kids were in the backyard sandpit,
I was more often than not on the floor of
my parents' fish-and-chip shop, being pulled
away to lend a hand. Work ethic and love of
food were never in doubt.

Mano

*South Perth,
Western Australia*

MEZZE PLATTER FAVOURITES

Recipe by *PETER MANIFIS*, Incontro, Western Australia, Australia

SERVINGS: 6–10 | PREP TIME: 45 MINS | COOK TIME: I HOUR | SKILL LEVEL: 2 (MODERATE)

INGREDIENTS

MINI SPANAKOPITA

For the filling

1 bunch spring onions, finely chopped
50 g butter
50 ml olive oil
1 bunch silverbeet, washed and chopped
100 g great-quality feta
50 g Kefalograviera (or haloumi if you can't find any), grated
5 eggs, lightly beaten

To finish

5 litres canola oil
8 sheets brik pastry
1 egg, beaten

KEFTEDES

300 g veal mince
1 cup mint, finely chopped
1 cup flat-leaf parsley, finely chopped
1 large brown onion, grated
4 large ripe tomatoes, grated
up to 1 cup water
up to 1 cup self-raising flour
400 ml canola oil,
   for shallow-frying

TARAMASALATA

300 g stale white bread, crusts removed
1 x 100 g can white tarama (salted, cured cod roe, available from most good delis)
¼ brown onion, roughly chopped
1 clove garlic, minced
juice of 2 lemons
¼ cup canola oil
⅓ cup olive oil
1 cup water

TO SERVE

3 small Lebanese cucumbers
6 pieces of fresh pita bread
200 g Kalamata olives
a handful of small, ripe tomatoes
a good few dollops of Greek yoghurt
good-quality olive oil

METHOD

For the mini spanakopita: in a large saucepan on a medium heat, lightly sauté the spring onion in the butter and olive oil until soft. Add in the silverbeet and cover the pan with a lid. Once the mixture has reduced by half, remove the pan from the heat, add the cheeses, eggs and freshly ground pepper to taste. Give everything a stir and set aside to cool.

Heat the canola oil to 180°C in a deep-fryer or a heavy-based pot. Take a sheet of brik pastry and place it onto a clean, damp tea towel. Brush the surface with a little beaten egg and then spoon a little of the mixture down the centre of the pastry sheet. Fold in the ends and roll the pastry like a cigar. Set aside on a tray in the freezer, and repeat until all of the pastry has been used. Freeze these filled pastry cigars for around 10 minutes prior to frying. Fry the cigars for about 2 minutes or until golden-brown and drain on paper towel.

For the keftedes: in a large mixing bowl, combine the mince, mint, parsley and grated onion and tomato, along with a good pinch of salt and pepper. Add about half a cup of water to the mix and then a ¼ cup of flour. Mix thoroughly. You can add a little more water or a little more flour depending on the texture of the mix – it should be slightly wet in the hand, but not sloppy. Form small, bite-sized patties and set aside until ready to cook.

To a heavy-based frying pan on a medium to high heat, add some canola oil and fry the patties for 2 minutes each side or until dark brown. Don't be scared of the mix going crispy – this adds a lovely texture to the keftedes.

Best eaten with Greek yoghurt (naturally!), these are fantastic consumed cold the next day.

For the taramasalata: briefly soak the bread in water and gently squeeze out excess liquid. Blitz the tarama, onion, garlic and softened bread in a blender. Add in most of the lemon juice and half of the oils and a good pinch of white pepper. Blitz again on a slow speed. Gradually add the rest of the oil, until smooth. Taste for seasoning, adding lemon or pepper as needed.

To serve, peel the cucumbers, quarter lengthwise and season with salt flakes. Serve the mini spanakopita, keftedes and taramasalata on a big platter with fresh pita bread, olives, halved tomatoes, cucumber and yoghurt. Drizzle the lot with olive oil, salt and ground pepper.

Oh – and don't forget the ouzo!

SAUSAGE, RADICCHIO & LEMON GNOCCHI

Recipe by JAMES MARTIN, chef & TV presenter, Yorkshire, England

SERVINGS: 4 | **PREP TIME: 30 MINS** | **COOK TIME: 2 HOURS** | **SKILL LEVEL: 2 (MODERATE)**

A great chef mate of mine — Stephen Terry — runs a fab place called The Hardwick in Abergavenny, Wales. If it's a nice day, I often take one of the old cars for a spin and go there for lunch. This was a dish I saw Stephen make and it's so good that I've nicked it both for this book and for me at home. It's very clever cooking from a top-class chef, using just a hint of spice, but the lemon calms it down. Trust me, you will like it.

INGREDIENTS

For the gnocchi

4 large floury potatoes

olive oil, for the potatoes

4 tbsp rock salt

75 g '00' flour, plus extra
   to dust

1 egg yolk

25 g Parmesan, finely grated

For the sauce

4 good-quality pork
   sausages, skins removed,
   roughly chopped

50 g unsalted butter

2 shallots, finely chopped

2 cloves garlic, finely
   chopped

1 tsp chilli flakes, or to taste

300 ml chicken stock

100 ml double cream

25 g capers, rinsed, roughly
   chopped

2 tbsp roughly chopped
   flat-leaf parsley leaves,
   plus more to serve

finely grated zest of
   2 unwaxed lemons

1 large head of radicchio,
   cut into wedges through
   the root

1 tbsp olive oil

50 g fresh white
   breadcrumbs

METHOD

For the gnocchi, pre-heat the oven to 170°C. Rub the potatoes with a little oil, then place on a small pile of rock salt on a baking tray. Bake in the oven for 1½ hours, or until tender. When cooked, remove from the oven and set aside until cool enough to handle.

Cut the potatoes in half and scoop out the flesh, then pass through a potato ricer or sieve into a large bowl. Add the flour and egg yolk, season, then mix lightly until it forms a soft dough. Tip onto a floured work surface, divide into quarters and roll each into a long sausage. Cut into 2 cm pieces and lightly pinch each in the middle.

Once all the gnocchi are cut, drop them into a large saucepan of boiling salted water. When the gnocchi bob to the surface, they are ready. Remove with a slotted spoon and place in a bowl of ice-cold water to cool.

To make the sauce, heat a frying pan until medium hot, add the sausage meat and half the butter and fry until golden-brown all over. Add the shallots, garlic and chilli flakes and cook for 2 minutes.

Pour in the chicken stock and simmer until it is reduced by half and the sausage meat is cooked through. Add the cream, drained gnocchi, capers, parsley and lemon zest and simmer for 2 minutes.

Heat a griddle pan until hot, toss the radicchio with the olive oil, then char on the griddle pan for 1 minute on each side.

Heat a small frying pan until medium hot, add the remaining butter and, when it's foaming, add the breadcrumbs and fry until golden. Season with salt and pepper. Tip the crumbs onto kitchen paper to cool.

Place the radicchio onto a serving plate, then spoon the gnocchi and sauce over the top. Finish with some Parmesan and a sprinkling of crunchy breadcrumbs.

PETA MATHIAS MNZM
CHEF & FOOD WRITER

I discovered when I was young that if you can cook, people will like you. Being able to cook means you can share something of yourself which doesn't cost anything. The magic of recipes is that they connect you to the past.

Duck confit is a great recipe from my French life. It's a good recipe for a dinner party because you can do the cooking the day before, then sauté it just before serving. Duck fat is not like any other fat; it gives food an unctuousness, a mouth-feel that is like nothing else. Putting duck fat and potatoes together is like dying and going to heaven.

Peta

Westmere,
Auckland

CONFIT DE CANARD
PRESERVED DUCK LEGS

Recipes by *PETA MATHIAS* MNZM, chef & food writer, Auckland, New Zealand

**SERVINGS: 6 | PREP TIME: 5 MINS PLUS MARINATING | COOK TIME: 2 HOURS PLUS MATURING
SKILL LEVEL: 1 (EASY)**

INGREDIENTS

6 duck legs

2 tbsp rock salt

1 tbsp crushed black peppercorns

2 cloves garlic, sliced

4 sprigs fresh thyme

2 bay leaves, crushed

2 litres melted duck fat

½ tsp ground white pepper

DF, GF

METHOD

Cover duck legs with all the ingredients except the fat and white pepper and marinate for 24 hours. Rinse the legs with cold water to remove the marinade.

Lie duck legs, skin-side down, in a large pot, add melted duck fat and white pepper and simmer very gently for 2 hours.

Allow to cool, then transfer legs and fat to an earthenware dish. Leave for at least a week in a cool place to mature before eating. The confit will keep in the fridge like that for up to two weeks. If you seal the pot with a salt-sprinkled cloth and then cover it with thick brown paper tied with string, the confit will keep for several months, either in a cool place or in the fridge.

To serve, allow the confit to sit in a warm place until the fat runs (this can be done in a gentle bain-marie). Drain the legs, then heat up a little of the duck fat in a frying pan and sauté the legs, skin-side down, until golden and crispy. Alternatively, grill them.

TIPS

In France, confit is usually served with sliced potatoes fried in duck fat (see below) and a salad. I suggest a chicory and dandelion salad splashed with walnut oil and tarragon vinegar.

Duck fat gives a creaminess and depth to dishes that is incomparable. It is all melted off during reheating, so try not to think of the fat transferring to your own legs! The fat can be strained and reused.

POMMES SARLADAISES
POTATOES IN DUCK FAT

SERVINGS: 6 | PREP TIME: 10 MINS | COOK TIME: 20–30 MINS | SKILL LEVEL: 1 (EASY)

INGREDIENTS

1 kg waxy potatoes (Désirée, Draga or Jersey Benne)

8 tbsp duck fat

2 cloves garlic, finely chopped

3 tbsp chopped fresh flat-leaf parsley

DF, GF

METHOD

Peel potatoes and slice very thinly. Dry with a tea towel. Melt half the duck fat, pour it into a bowl, add salt and pepper and toss the potato slices in it.

Heat the rest of the duck fat in a large, heavy-based frying pan. Tip the potatoes in and cook on medium heat for about 10 minutes to get a golden base. Now start moving the slices around so that other layers can take on some colour. When they are all golden and cooked through, you can either stir in the garlic and parsley and serve, or serve and scatter the garlic and parsley over the top.

MEGAN MAY
LITTLE BIRD UNBAKERY

Little Bird came from me trying to feed and heal myself as I've always had allergies and ended up seriously ill and unable to work. My philosophy is that we should be eating foods that make our bodies feel good, whatever they might be. It's about health. Everybody should eat some raw food every day and most people have a salad or a fresh piece of fruit, which is great. Raw foods generally make people feel better and more energised – who doesn't want that?

Megan

Kingsland,
Auckland

CASHEW & MACADAMIA MILK

Recipes by MEGAN MAY, Little Bird Unbakery, Auckland, New Zealand

MAKES: 500 ML | **PREP TIME: 5 MINS PLUS SOAKING** | **SKILL LEVEL: 1 (EASY)**

INGREDIENTS

⅓ cup cashew nuts
¼ cup macadamia nuts
2 cups filtered water
pinch of salt
pinch of vanilla paste or
  1 tsp vanilla extract

DF, GF, V

METHOD

Soak cashew and macadamia nuts separately in cold water for 2–4 hours. Drain.

Next, blend all ingredients on high in a regular blender or a VitaMix for 1–2 minutes. Strain through a cheesecloth or a nut milk bag, and place in a sealed jar or bottle.

Keeps in the fridge for two days.

TIPS

When dairy is off the menu, nut milks make a wonderful substitute or addition to your repertoire. Cashews are one of the creamiest of nuts and, when mixed with macadamias, the taste of the nut milk is even closer to the dairy flavour people are familiar with. You can use it in almost any way you would regularly use dairy milk.

RASPBERRY MILKSHAKE (HOLD THE MILK)

SERVINGS: 2 | **PREP TIME: 5 MINS** | **SKILL LEVEL: 1 (EASY)**

INGREDIENTS

1 cup cashew and
  macadamia milk
  (see recipe above)
1 cup ice cubes
1 banana, frozen
2 tbsp raw agave syrup,
  organic maple syrup or
  raw honey
½ tsp vanilla extract
¼ cup frozen raspberries,
  plus extra to serve

DF, GF, V

METHOD

Blend all the ingredients except the raspberries in a high-speed blender until smooth. Pour half the smoothie mixture into two glasses (leaving half in the blender).

To the remaining mixture in the blender, add half the frozen raspberries and blend until the mixture is a lovely pink colour. Pour half of the contents into each glass to create berries and cream.

To finish, lightly crush a few extra raspberries and sprinkle on top.

TIP

While not your typical milkshake, this does taste like a familiar Kiwi favourite, reminiscent of a jelly-tip ice cream — but without any gluten, milk or sugary substances or those additives you can't recognise the names of which are present in most milkshakes or ice creams.

MUM'S SWEETCORN FRITTERS

Recipe by *ANDREW McCONNELL*, Cutler & Co, Victoria, Australia

SERVINGS: 4-6 | PREP TIME: 10 MINS | COOK TIME: 20-25 MINS | SKILL LEVEL: 1 (EASY)

INGREDIENTS

1 sweetcorn on the cob
1 x 310 g can creamed corn
1 egg
3 spring onions, thinly sliced
pinch of ground cumin
pinch of ground white pepper
3 tbsp self-raising flour
butter and oil, for cooking

V

METHOD

Plunge the corn cob into a pot of boiling water for 4 minutes. Drain, then cut the kernels from the cob with a sharp knife.

Combine the corn kernels, creamed corn, egg, spring onion and spices in a bowl and whisk well. Sieve the flour into the bowl, along with salt to taste, and beat into a batter.

To test the batter, heat a non-stick frying pan with a teaspoon of oil and a little butter. When the butter has melted, add 1 tablespoon of the batter. Cook over a moderate heat for 2–3 minutes until golden, then flip the fritter and continue to cook for a few minutes more. A little extra flour can be added to the batter if the fritter is not holding together.

Fry the fritters in batches, adding a little extra oil and butter to the pan as necessary.

ANGUS MCINTOSH
FARMER ANGUS

Although I grew up on a farm, I never intended
to become a farmer. Michael Pollan's book
The Omnivore's Dilemma changed all that.
Our regenerative farming is enabled by lots of
different animals. These recipes are celebrations
of our pastures: a bone broth (a tonic that has
been linked with helping to cure myriad diseases)
and, of course, biltong — one of South Africa's
most iconic food products. *Angus*

Stellenbosch,
Western Cape

BONE BROTH

Recipes by *ANGUS McINTOSH*, Farmer Angus, Western Cape, South Africa

MAKES: 4 LITRES (APPROX.) | **PREP TIME: 15 MINS PLUS SOAKING** | **COOK TIME: 30 HOURS (APPROX.)**
SKILL LEVEL: 1 (EASY)

INGREDIENTS

2 kg grass-fed beef bones
6 litres filtered rainwater
2 tbsp vinegar
2 carrots, roughly chopped
1 onion, cut in half
1 sprig rosemary
1 celery stalk
1 clove garlic
2 tsp ground turmeric
1 tsp black peppercorns
2 bay leaves

DF, GF

METHOD

Cover the bones in rainwater and vinegar and leave to soak for 2 hours. Bring to a slow simmer, just below boiling point. Scoop off any scum that rises to the top. Add carrot, onion, rosemary, celery, garlic, turmeric, peppercorns and bay leaves. Simmer slowly for 26–28 hours. Allow to cool with the bones in the broth (about another 3 hours). Remove bones and scoop off any fat from the top, then bottle and keep in the fridge. Drink it neat or use as a base for soups or risottos.

BILTONG

MAKES: ABOUT 1KG (APPROX.) | **PREP TIME: 5 MINS PLUS SOAKING & DRYING** | **SKILL LEVEL: 1 (EASY)**

INGREDIENTS

2 kg grass-fed beef
(preferably silverside)
150 ml very good vinegar
2 tbsp coarse salt
2 tbsp coriander seeds,
roasted and crushed

DF, GF

METHOD

The drying process can take anything from 24 hours to 5 days, depending on where you hang the meat, so start at least 1–2 days before. Cut the meat into 2 cm slices (about 20 cm in length, depending on your cut of meat). Mix together the vinegar, salt and coriander seeds in a glass or non-metallic dish. Soak the beef overnight in the vinegar mixture, in the fridge. Remove meat from the vinegar mixture and hang to dry in a space free of flies and ideally with a fan moving the air. It's important to keep the biltong free from humidity.

Fremantle,
Western Australia

JIM MENDOLIA
FREMANTLE SARDINES

I was brought up in an Italian fishing family and just love it. Every morning we get up before dawn to chase Sardines. The dolphins come out, we watch the sunrise; there's really nothing like it.

Jim

MUM'S FRIED SARDINES WITH HERBED MAYONNAISE

Recipe by *JIM MENDOLIA*, Fremantle Sardines, Western Australia, Australia

SERVINGS: 6 | **PREP TIME: 20–40 MINS** | **COOK TIME: 10–15 MINS** | **SKILL LEVEL: 1 (EASY)**

INGREDIENTS

4 cups fresh breadcrumbs

¾ cup grated Parmesan

2 tbsp chopped parsley,
  plus extra for garnish

24 sardines, cleaned and
  boned linguetta fashion
  (butterfly-style fillet; can
  be bought ready-prepared)

1 cup plain flour

2 eggs

4 tbsp milk

olive oil for frying

lemon wedges to serve

Herbed mayonnaise

¾ cup good-quality mayonnaise

1 tbsp chopped parsley

1 finely chopped shallot

3 tsp chopped capers

1 tbsp chopped gherkins

METHOD

Herbed mayonnaise: combine all the ingredients, mixing well and seasoning with salt and freshly ground black pepper.

Sardines: combine breadcrumbs, Parmesan, parsley, and salt and freshly ground black pepper to taste. Place in a wide, shallow bowl.

Place flour in another wide, shallow bowl. Beat eggs with milk in a third wide, shallow bowl.

Open sardines flat and coat lightly with flour, dip in combined egg and milk, then coat well with breadcrumb mixture.

Heat oil in a frying pan and cook sardines on both sides until golden-brown and cooked through – approximately 2 minutes each side.

Serve hot with herbed mayonnaise and lemon wedges. Garnish with extra parsley.

OKA I'A

RAW FISH & COCONUT SALAD

Recipe by *MICHAEL MEREDITH*, Meredith's, Auckland, New Zealand

SERVINGS: 4 | PREP TIME: 45 MINS | SKILL LEVEL: I (EASY)

I spent my early childhood in the Pacific Islands, which gave me a respect for ingredients and the experience of working with raw materials. I came to New Zealand as a teenager and was exposed to the diversity of its culture. All these things, along with travelling, are reflected in the way I cook.

INGREDIENTS

300 g raw fish (tuna, mahi mahi or tarakihi)
200 g cucumber
100 g spring onions
150 g green coconut flesh
2 cups fresh coconut cream
lemon juice, to taste
salt, to taste
1 red or green chilli
3 medium-sized tomatoes
½ cup chopped coriander leaves

DF, GF

METHOD

Cut fish into 2 cm chunks, chop cucumber into large dice, slice spring onions and dice coconut. Place in a non-metallic bowl.

In another bowl, make the dressing. Mix coconut cream, lemon juice and salt. Finely chop chilli and mix in. Pour onto the fish and gently mix. Adjust seasoning and also make up and add more dressing if you want.

Chop tomatoes and stir in. Let it sit for 20 minutes in the fridge before eating. Lightly mix chopped coriander in before serving.

TRADITIONAL ROAST RIB OF BEEF

Recipe by *PIPPA MIDDLETON*, food enthusiast, London, England

SERVINGS: 8 | **PREP TIME: 15 MINS PLUS RESTING** | **COOK TIME: VARIES** | **SKILL LEVEL: 1 (EASY)**

The ultimate Sunday lunch dish, roast beef and Yorkshire pudding is a quintessential British combination, well known from the middle of the 18th century when the French started referring to the English as 'les rosbifs'. Rib of beef is one of the tastiest cuts as it's cooked on the bone, which also makes for a flavoursome gravy. Ask the butcher to trim the bones for a neat finish. I like to cheat a little and use shop-bought fresh or frozen Yorkshire puddings. Remember to remove the meat from the fridge half an hour before cooking to allow it to come to room temperature.

INGREDIENTS

3- to 4-bone trimmed rib of beef, 3 kg (approx.)
4–6 tbsp Dijon mustard

For the horseradish sauce
100 g hot horseradish sauce
4 tbsp crème fraîche
a squeeze of lemon juice

For the gravy
4 tbsp plain flour
800 ml good-quality beef stock
200 ml red wine

METHOD

Pre-heat the oven to 220°C. Place the rib of beef in a large roasting tray and spread the mustard all over the meat. Season well with salt and pepper. Roast in the pre-heated oven for 20 minutes, then reduce the heat to 170°C and roast for the remaining calculated cooking time (see roasting times below). Baste occasionally with the roasting juices. Once the meat is cooked to your preference, remove it from the oven, transfer it to a board and cover with foil. Reserve the roasting juices. Allow the meat to rest for at least 25–30 minutes. Combine the horseradish sauce, crème fraîche and lemon juice in a bowl. Season to taste.

To make the gravy, drain all but 3–4 tablespoons of fat from the roasting tray. Place the tray on the hob over a medium heat and stir in the flour. Once combined, gradually whisk in the stock and red wine. Continue to whisk until smooth and allow to reduce until thickened. Season with salt and pepper to taste, add the roasting juices and strain before serving. Serve with a red claret, accompanied by the horseradish sauce and gravy.

ROASTING TIMES FOR BEEF ON THE BONE

For rare, allow 12 minutes per 450 grams, plus 15 minutes.

For medium-rare, allow 16 minutes per 450 grams, plus 20 minutes.

For well done, allow 20 minutes per 450 grams, plus 25 minutes.

Check and baste the meat frequently and adjust the timings for your particular oven.

LYNDEY MILAN OAM
CHEF, FOOD WRITER & TV PRESENTER

Comfort food is, of course, different to different people and it is
especially different for different cultures. Personally, I think you should
eat comfort food with one hand. Nothing formal, just a fork will do.

*Waverton,
New South Wales*

MEATLOAF WITH ITALIAN FLAVOURS

Recipe by *LYNDEY MILAN OAM*, chef, food writer & TV presenter, New South Wales, Australia

SERVINGS: 6 | PREP TIME: 15 MINS | COOK TIME: 1 HOUR | SKILL LEVEL: 1 (EASY)

INGREDIENTS

250 g Italian sausages

1 large (350 g) red capsicum, chopped finely

1 large (200 g) brown onion, chopped finely

4 cloves garlic, chopped finely

500 g beef mince

100 g sliced salami or chorizo, coarsely chopped

½ cup good-quality pitted black olives, halved

¾ cup (50 g) fresh breadcrumbs

⅓ cup (80 ml) good-quality barbecue sauce

2 eggs, beaten lightly

¼ cup flat-leaf parsley, chopped finely

125 g cherry tomatoes, halved

1 x 400 g can diced tomatoes

basil leaves, for garnish

salad or seasonal green vegetables, to serve

DF

METHOD

Pre-heat oven to 200°C.

Line a 1½ litre loaf tin (e.g. 20 cm x 12 cm x 8 cm) with plastic wrap to mould meatloaf in. Using baking paper, line a baking tray big enough to hold the loaf tin (a lamington tray is perfect).

Remove sausages from their skins, crumble and, in a large bowl, combine with capsicum, onion, garlic, beef mince, salami or chorizo, olives, breadcrumbs, barbecue sauce, egg and parsley. Press this mixture tightly into the loaf tin, then turn it out onto the baking dish and remove the loaf tin which has acted as a mould. Combine cherry and canned tomatoes and pour evenly over the meatloaf.

Bake meatloaf, uncovered, for about 1 hour or until cooked through. If the cherry tomatoes start to burn, cover with tinfoil. Stand for 10 minutes before cutting. Serve with salad or steamed vegetables, as desired.

Bo-Kaap,
Western Cape

KUBRA MOHAMED
COMMUNITY BAKER

Every Saturday for the past 18 years, I've been cooking koesisters for the people of the Bo-Kaap community in Cape Town. My first customers arrive at about 4 a.m., after mosque, so I have everything prepared and ready. They line up in the street and then in my passageway, bringing along their plates and weekend chatter. Feeding my community on the weekend is incredibly important to me, and I'll carry on as long as I can.

Kubra

KOESISTERS

Recipe by *KUBRA MOHAMED*, community baker, Western Cape, South Africa

MAKES: 70–80 (SMALL) | **PREP TIME: 20 MINS PLUS RESTING & RISING** | **COOK TIME: 20 MINS**
SKILL LEVEL: 2 (MODERATE)

INGREDIENTS

1 cup sugar
125 g soft butter
1½ cups boiling water
1 cup milk
1 tbsp fine cinnamon
1 tbsp elachi (cardamom)
1 tbsp fine dried ginger
1 tbsp mixed spice
1 tsp fine aniseed
2 tsp ground naartjie peel
   (see tip)
20 g instant yeast
1 egg
1 kg flour
vegetable oil, for
   deep-frying
2 cups desiccated
   coconut, for sprinkling

For the syrup
4 cups water
3 cups sugar
2 strips dried naartjie peel
   (see note)

V

METHOD

Place the sugar and butter in a bowl, add rapidly boiling water and milk, and mix well. Add in the spices, yeast and egg, and mix well again. Add the flour to form a dough, then knead it until it's smooth and allow it to rest for an hour.

Make the syrup by combining the ingredients in a pot and bringing the mixture to a slow simmer.

Roll the dough into 'sausages', then cut them into 5 cm pieces and make the ends rounded. Leave the koesisters to rise for 15 minutes.

Deep-fry the koesisters on a medium heat until dark brown on the outside. Prick the koesisters and place in the syrup in the pot. Simmer for 5 minutes on each side, remove and sprinkle with coconut.

TIP

To make dried naartjie powder, sun-dry 10 naartjie peels for two days until very dry. Store the dried peel in an airtight container until needed (it must stay totally dry to avoid mould). Grind to a fine powder in a coffee grinder just before using.

NOTE

My recipe is simple and has taken many years to perfect. Naartjies are a type of mandarin or tangerine and are so prolific towards the end of winter, so that's the best time to buy in bulk. We dry the skins in the hot African sun. Once the skins are totally dried out, I blend them in a coffee grinder to a fine powder. This produces a naartjie flavour that is incredibly sweet and citrusy, and I think this is what I would call my secret ingredient! It adds another depth of flavour to basic bread dough, and lends itself to the other spices we use in the koesisters.

PAN-FRIED BARRAMUNDI WITH A SALAD OF RAW ZUCCHINI & FRESH HERBS

Recipe by *MATT MORAN*, chef & restaurateur, Australia

SERVINGS: 4 | PREP TIME: 15 MINS | COOK TIME: 10 MINS | SKILL LEVEL: 1 (EASY)

Bondi Beach, to me, is one of the best places on earth. There's nothing better than finishing work, if you get the night off, coming down here right on twilight, having a swim and then having a cold beer. And when you think of the beach, you think of fresh seafood. barbecued prawns and barramundi: it's seafood at its best.

INGREDIENTS

2 green zucchini
2 yellow zucchini or squash
¼ bunch mint leaves
  (reserve some for garnish)
¼ bunch parsley leaves

For the dressing
½ clove garlic, finely chopped
zest and juice of 1 lemon
  (reserve some for garnish)
100 ml olive oil
4 x 180 g ocean barramundi
  fillets, skin on
1 tbsp olive oil
sea salt flakes
1 tbsp vegetable oil for frying
4 tbsp white wine
4 baby zucchini flowers
¼ bunch dill, picked into sprigs

DF, GF

METHOD

Using a mandolin, shave the zucchini (or squash) into long thin strips, and place in a bowl with the mint and parsley.

Make the dressing by whisking together the garlic and the lemon zest and juice, then slowly adding the olive oil until combined.

Pat the fillets dry with a paper towel and, using a sharp knife, lightly score the skin enough to go through the skin but not cut into the flesh. Season with olive oil and a good pinch of sea salt.

In a heavy-based frying pan on a medium to high heat, add a tablespoon of vegetable oil and, after a few seconds, place the fillets in the pan, skin-side down. Use a fish slice or spatula to press the fillets flat to the pan to avoid the fillets curling. After 2–3 minutes, or when the skin is crisp and golden, flip the fillets and cook the other side for a further 2 minutes or until just cooked. Remove the fillets from the pan and set aside.

Dress the zucchini and season to taste with salt and freshly ground black pepper. Arrange the salad on the four plates with the fish fillets, and garnish with the dill sprigs, mint leaves and a squeeze of fresh lemon.

SIBA MTONGANA
AUTHOR & CELEBRITY CHEF

Growing up in Mdantsane, we cooked traditional food —
always rice or samp and beans, meat, gravy and at least
three vegetables. But don't be fooled — these simple
ingredients saw so many new variations that it was
possible to believe that my mother was a magician. This
is really the crux of it: food is all about family and friends,
and putting your heart into preparing a meal is the same
as presenting them with a wonderful gift. Food prepared
with care says, 'I love you'.

Siba

Cape Town,
Western Cape

PAPIZZA

Recipe by *SIBA MTONGANA*, author & celebrity chef, Western Cape, South Africa

SERVINGS: 4 | **PREP TIME: 10 MINS** | **COOK TIME: 40 MINS** | **SKILL LEVEL: 1 (EASY)**

INGREDIENTS

750 ml water
pinch of salt
530 g maize meal
30 g butter
125 ml basil or rocket
  pesto
30 ml sweet chilli sauce
225 g chorizo, sliced
½ red onion, sliced
150 g broccolini, blanched
  (see tip)
300 ml shaved Parmesan
rocket, to garnish
  (optional)

GF

METHOD

Pre-heat the oven to 220°C. In a medium-sized saucepan, bring the water and salt to a rapid boil. Add half the maize meal and whisk to remove lumps. Reduce heat to medium, stir with a wooden spoon and cook, covered, for 8 minutes. Stir again and add the remaining maize meal, a little at a time, stirring and repeatedly mashing it against the sides of the saucepan with the back of the wooden spoon to prevent lumps from forming. This will take about 5 minutes. Reduce heat further and cook for 15–20 minutes until the mixture has thickened to a stiff consistency and is cooked. Add butter and mix. Cool slightly. Flatten into a pizza pan to create a pizza base.

Smear the papizza base with half the pesto and all the sweet chilli sauce. Scatter with chorizo, onion, broccolini, the remaining pesto and Parmesan. Season and bake for 10 minutes, or until cheese has melted. Remove from the oven and garnish with rocket, if using. Slice and serve warm.

TIPS

Broccolini is often sold as tenderstem broccoli. To blanch it, bring a pot of salted water to the boil, add the broccolini, cook for 2 minutes and remove to a colander. Rinse with cold water and drain.

You'll need a pizza lifter or fish slice to lift the pizza slices, as the papizza will be soft when warm.

XOLISWA NDOYIYA
NELSON MANDELA'S PRIVATE CHEF

This chicken dish reminds you of who you are and where you grew up. It was Mr Mandela's favourite and he always asked for his gravy on the side. If it wasn't there, he would call me and say, 'Xoli, where is my gravy? Wasn't the bird drinking anything?'

Xoliswa

*Queenstown,
Eastern Cape*

UMLEQWA

FARM CHICKEN

Recipe by *XOLISWA NDOYIYA*, Nelson Mandela's private chef, Eastern Cape, South Africa

SERVINGS: 4 | PREP TIME: 15 MINS | COOK TIME: 35 MINS | SKILL LEVEL: 1 (EASY)

INGREDIENTS

1½ kg chicken (farm is best but otherwise free range), cut into pieces
1 onion, chopped
1 tbsp flour
3 cups (750 ml) chicken stock
chopped fresh parsley, to serve

DF

METHOD

Season the chicken with salt and pepper. Boil the chicken in 1 cup water for 10 minutes with the lid off; the water will evaporate. Allow the chicken to slightly fry in its own fat for a further 5 minutes. Add the onion and flour, and cook for another few minutes. Stir in the stock, bring to the boil and cover. Cook for 20–25 minutes until the chicken has cooked through.

Scatter with parsley, and serve with the sauce on the side.

RUSSELL NORMAN
CHEF & RESTAURATEUR

I really like this burrata dish because it's quite proletarian. Burrata is basically mozzarella with the addition of cream, lentils are the staple that you have on any larder shelf gathering dust, and basil's just one of those beautiful, fresh herbs that's now available throughout the year. It's a very simple recipe with very simple and uncomplicated ingredients — yet the combination of those flavours creates one of those dishes that makes me smile.

Soho,
London

Russell

BURRATA WITH LENTILS & BASIL OIL

Recipe by *RUSSELL NORMAN*, chef & restaurateur, London, England

SERVINGS: 6 | **PREP TIME: 20 MINS** | **COOK TIME: 55 MINS** | **SKILL LEVEL: 2 (MODERATE)**

Burrata is often confused with mozzarella, but they are not the same. Burrata is made in Puglia with milk from razza Podolica cows (not buffalo) and with added cream, so it is softer and more moist than mozzarella. Burrata's creamy, sweet consistency is the perfect foil to an array of ingredients. It is a delight with bitter cime di rapa (turnip tops), for example. This recipe combines it with lentils – a heavenly marriage. Make sure that your burrata is of the finest quality and at room temperature. Serving it fridge-cold kills the texture and the flavour.

INGREDIENTS

For the basil oil
leaves from a bunch of basil
flaky sea salt and black pepper
extra virgin olive oil

400 g Puy lentils
2 large carrots, finely chopped
3 sticks celery, finely chopped
1 small onion, finely chopped
3 cloves garlic, finely chopped
5 sprigs thyme, leaves removed and chopped
6 burrata balls

For the mustard dressing (you'll only need 4 tbsp of this)
100 ml extra virgin olive oil
25 ml red wine vinegar
1 tbsp Dijon mustard
1 tsp caster sugar

GF, V

METHOD

First make the basil oil by placing most of the basil leaves in a food processor, reserving a few of the smaller, prettier ones for decorating at the end. Add a little salt and enough olive oil to make a thin sauce. Whizz for a few seconds then set aside.

Put the lentils in a saucepan with enough cold water to cover them by about 7 cm. Don't add salt at this stage, as this will toughen the lentils. Bring to the boil and cook for about 45 minutes. Keep checking them – they need to still hold a small bite. When they are done, drain, refresh in cold water, drain again and set aside.

Now, in a large heavy-based pan sweat the vegetables in a few good glugs of olive oil with the thyme leaves, a large pinch of salt and a twist of ground black pepper. When the vegetables are softened and translucent, add the cooked lentils and a splash of water to stop them sticking to the bottom of the pan.

Make the mustard dressing. Put the olive oil, red wine vinegar, Dijon mustard, a small pinch of salt, a couple of grinds of pepper and the sugar into a bowl and whisk together.

To finish the dish, add 4 tablespoons of the mustard dressing to the lentils, check the seasoning and spoon onto a large warm plate. Then tear open your burrata and place on top of the warm lentils. The heat from the lentils will melt the burrata, making it even more creamy and soft.

Drizzle some basil oil over the top and scatter with the reserved basil leaves.

NATALIE OLDFIELD
COOK & AUTHOR

Food and love have always gone together for me.
I remember that, when I was a little girl, so much
of my family life revolved around two places –
Gran's kitchen and Gran's table. My own cooking
started because I watched my gran from an early
age. She taught me the value of food in showing
love by giving to others – no matter who it was,
she would share food with them, including us, her
grandchildren. Never a birthday went by that my
gran didn't give us some peanut brownies and she
often made Louise cake for our afternoon tea.
I love baking them because they bring back such
wonderful memories.

Natalie

Remuera,
Auckland

PEANUT BROWNIES

Recipes by NATALIE OLDFIELD, cook & author, Auckland, New Zealand

MAKES: ABOUT 24 | PREP TIME: 20–25 MINS | COOK TIME: 20–25 MINS | SKILL LEVEL: 1 (EASY)

INGREDIENTS

250 g butter, softened
2 cups sugar
2 eggs
2 tsp vanilla essence
2 cups plain flour
2 tbsp cocoa
½ tsp salt
1 tsp baking powder
2½ cups roasted peanuts
1 cup coconut

V

METHOD

Pre-heat the oven to 170°C. Grease and line a baking tray.

Cream butter and sugar together until light and fluffy. Add eggs one at a time, beating well after each addition, then add vanilla and combine. Sift in flour, cocoa, salt and baking powder. Fold to combine. Lastly, add roasted peanuts and coconut. Mix together well.

Roll mixture into tablespoon-sized balls and press to flatten slightly when placing on baking tray. Bake for 20–25 minutes. Cool on a rack.

TIP

To roast your own peanuts, put them in a baking dish in an oven pre-heated to 120°C for 20 minutes, shaking them occasionally. You can keep their skins on – they're not too husky for this recipe.

LOUISE CAKE

SERVINGS: 16 | PREP TIME: 15–20 MINS | COOK TIME: 20–25 MINS | SKILL LEVEL: 1 (EASY)

INGREDIENTS

For the cake
150 g butter, softened
¼ cup white sugar
2 egg yolks
2 cups self-raising flour
¾ cup raspberry jam

For the meringue
2 egg whites
½ cup sugar
1½ cups coconut

V

METHOD

Pre-heat the oven to 180°C. Grease and line a 30 cm x 20 cm slice tin.

Cream butter and sugar together until light and fluffy, then add egg yolks and beat well. Sift flour and stir in, then use your hands to achieve an even consistency.

Press mixture into slice tin, then spread jam over the top.

To make the meringue, beat egg whites and sugar until thick, then fold in coconut. Spread the meringue on top of the jam and cake.

Bake for 20–25 minutes. Cool in the tin before slicing.

TIPS

Don't be afraid to get your hands into this when preparing the base!

When spreading the meringue over the top, you can use a hot knife to help.

FANTASTIC FISH PIE

Recipe by *JAMIE OLIVER MBE*, chef & TV presenter, Essex, England

SERVINGS: 6 | PREP TIME: 25 MINS | COOK TIME: 50 MINS | SKILL LEVEL: 1 (EASY)

The whole fish pie thing is one of the most homely, comforting and moreish dinners I can think of. This is a cracking recipe which does it for me.

INGREDIENTS

5 large potatoes, peeled and diced into 2½ cm squares

2 free-range eggs

2 large handfuls fresh spinach

1 onion, finely chopped

1 carrot, halved and finely chopped

extra virgin olive oil

285 ml double cream (approx.)

2 good handfuls grated mature Cheddar or Parmesan

juice of 1 lemon

1 heaped tsp English mustard

1 large handful flat-leaf parsley, finely chopped

455 g haddock or cod fillets, skin removed, pin-boned and sliced into strips

ground or freshly grated nutmeg (optional)

GF

METHOD

Pre-heat the oven to 230°C. Put the potatoes into salted boiling water and bring back to the boil for 2 minutes. Carefully add the eggs to the pan and cook for a further 8 minutes until hard-boiled, by which time the potatoes should also be cooked. At the same time, steam the spinach in a colander above the pan. This will only take a minute. When the spinach is done, remove from the colander and gently squeeze any excess moisture away. Then drain the potatoes in the colander. Remove the eggs, cool under cold water, then peel and quarter them. Place to one side.

In a separate pan, slowly fry the onion and carrot in a little olive oil for about 5 minutes, then add the double cream and bring just to the boil. Remove from the heat and add the cheese, lemon juice, mustard and parsley. Put the spinach, fish and eggs into an appropriately sized earthenware dish and mix together, pouring over the creamy vegetable sauce. The cooked potatoes should be drained and mashed – add a bit of olive oil, salt, pepper and a touch of nutmeg if you like. Spread on top of the fish. Don't bother piping it to look pretty – it's a homely hearty thing.

Place in the oven for about 25–30 minutes until the potatoes are golden. Serve with some nice peas or greens, not forgetting your baked beans and tomato ketchup. Tacky but tasty and that's what I like.

PEA & MINT CROQUETTES

Recipe by *YOTAM OTTOLENGHI*, Nopi, London, England

SERVINGS: 4 | **PREP TIME: 45 MINS PLUS FREEZING** | **COOK TIME: 40 MINS** | **SKILL LEVEL: 2 (MODERATE)**

For a while, we had a pretty wicked trio running the evening service at Ottolenghi in Islington. Tom, Sam and Myles were notorious for working hard and playing hard — in so many senses — but unfortunately the whiteness of this page prevents me from disclosing any details. All three had two things in common: a cheeky, irresistible grin, and an unusual passion for what they cooked. These croquettes are their creation and worth a little effort. They can be made well in advance and taken up to the stage where they are covered in panko breadcrumbs and frozen. You can then partially defrost and fry them as you need. The recipe makes 16 generously-sized patties, ample for four people. To feed more, or to serve as a snack or starter, make them into smaller croquettes, weighing about 40 grams each.

INGREDIENTS

3 tbsp olive oil

6 banana shallots, finely chopped (approx. 300 g)

1 tbsp white wine vinegar

700 g frozen and defrosted peas

20 g mint leaves, finely shredded

1 clove garlic, crushed

4 eggs

100 g plain flour

150 g panko breadcrumbs

sunflower oil, for frying

For the sauce

1 tsp dried mint

120 g sour cream

1 tbsp olive oil

V

METHOD

To make the sauce, place all the ingredients in a bowl with ¼ teaspoon salt and a grind of black pepper. Mix well and refrigerate until ready to use.

Place the olive oil in a medium sauté pan on a medium heat. Add the shallots and sauté for 15–20 minutes, stirring often, until soft. Add the vinegar, cook for a further 2 minutes and then remove from the heat.

Place the peas in a food processor and briefly blitz. They need to break down without turning into a mushy paste. Transfer to a mixing bowl and stir in the shallots, mint, garlic, 1 egg, ½ teaspoon salt and plenty of black pepper.

Line a tray that will fit in your freezer with baking parchment and shape the pea mixture into 16 patties (around 60 grams), about 7 cm across and 2 cm thick. Freeze for a couple of hours to firm up.

Place the remaining eggs in a bowl and gently beat. Place the flour in a separate bowl and the breadcrumbs in a third. Remove the croquettes from the freezer and, at one time, roll them in the flour, dip them in the egg, then coat them in the crumbs. You can then either return them to the freezer at this point or leave them at room temperature for about 1 hour, until partly defrosted. Whatever you do, it's important, when it comes to frying, that the patties are not entirely frozen; you want them to cook through without burning the crust.

Pre-heat the oven to 220°C/200°C fan.

Fill a medium-sized frying pan with enough sunflower oil so that it comes 2½ cm up the sides. Place on a medium–high heat and leave for 5 minutes for the oil to get hot. Reduce the heat to medium and fry the croquettes in batches for about 4 minutes, turning once, until both sides are golden-brown.

Transfer to a baking tray and place in the oven for 5 minutes, to warm through. Serve at once, with the sauce spooned on top or served alongside.

RICHARD OUSBY
STOKEHOUSE Q BRISBANE

When I moved into this house, the first thing I wanted to do was to plant a veggie garden. When there's nothing in the fridge you can always go out the back, rip a few things out of the ground, toss them together with whatever condiments you have in the cupboard and it's all you really need.

Richard

Stafford,
Queensland

STICKY MEAT SOUP
HEARTY BRAISED LAMB SHANKS

Recipe by *RICHARD OUSBY*, Stokehouse Q, Queensland, Australia

SERVINGS: 5 | PREP TIME: 30 MINS | COOK TIME: 2 HOURS | SKILL LEVEL: I (EASY)

INGREDIENTS

2 onions, chopped
2 large carrots
4 sticks celery
2 large leeks,
  green tops removed
3 cloves garlic
50 ml olive oil
5 lamb shanks
100 ml white wine
3 litres chicken stock
2 sprigs thyme
1 bay leaf
handful of parsley

DF, GF

METHOD

Pre-heat the oven to 150°C.

Peel all the vegetables and cut into large (50-cent size) pieces.

Heat olive oil in the bottom of a casserole dish and brown the shanks. This can be done in batches if space in the dish is a problem. After 5 minutes, or when the shanks are golden-brown, remove them from the dish.

In the same dish, sauté the onion, carrot, celery, leek and garlic until the onion goes clear.

Add the shanks back to the pot and deglaze with the white wine, reducing the wine until it is almost gone. Add the chicken stock, thyme, 2 good pinches of salt and the bay leaf. Bring to a simmer. Place in the oven for 2 hours, until the lamb is very soft and falling off the bone.

Season the soup with salt, pepper and parsley. Carefully spoon one shank into each serving bowl, then divide the vegetables and broth evenly among them. Serve with sliced crusty bread smeared with butter.

NATHAN OUTLAW
RESTAURANT NATHAN OUTLAW

I'm a seafood chef, and my philosophy is to keep food simple, seasonal and local. This is a lovely grilled John Dory with curry sauce and a little bit of cabbage and a few pickled onions. A very, very simple recipe that I hope you'll like.

Port Isaac,
Cornwall

JOHN DORY WITH CURRY SAUCE, CABBAGE & SHALLOTS

Recipe by *NATHAN OUTLAW*, Restaurant Nathan Outlaw, Cornwall, England

**SERVINGS: 4 | PREP TIME: 45 MINS PLUS CHILLING & OVERNIGHT INFUSING | COOK TIME: 35 MINS
SKILL LEVEL: 2 (MODERATE)**

Using a mayonnaise-based sauce is a good way to get flavours into a dish without overpowering the taste of the fish. John Dory has a lovely delicate flavour, which is enhanced here by a subtle, fresh-tasting curry sauce. Buttery cabbage and shallots contrast the moist texture of the fish beautifully.

INGREDIENTS

1 savoy or hispi cabbage
75 g (2½ oz) unsalted butter
2 large banana shallots, peeled and thinly sliced
2 John Dory, about 600 g each, gutted, filleted, skinned and pin-boned

For the curry sauce
2 medium-sized egg yolks
1 tsp mild curry powder
3 tsp white wine vinegar
200 ml sunflower oil
75 ml apple juice

*For the curry oil
(makes about 400 ml)*
4 tsp mild curry powder
400 ml light rapeseed oil

GF

METHOD

First make the curry oil. Sprinkle the curry powder into a dry frying pan and toast over a medium heat for 1–2 minutes until it releases its aroma; don't let it burn. Pour the oil into the pan and remove from the heat. Give it a good stir and then pour it into a jug. Leave to infuse and settle for 24 hours, then decant the curry oil into another container. It will keep for three months in a dark cupboard.

Bring a large saucepan of lightly salted water to the boil. Remove and set aside 6–12 large outer leaves from the cabbage (you may need fewer for the sausage, depending on the size of your cabbage); halve, core and shred the rest.

Add the whole cabbage leaves to the boiling water and blanch for 2 minutes. Remove and drain thoroughly, then plunge into ice-cold water to refresh, then drain and set aside.

Heat the butter in a pan over a medium heat. When hot, add the shallots and shredded cabbage and cook for 3 minutes to soften, then tip onto a tray, spread out and leave to cool.

Lay a sheet of clingfilm on your work surface. Lay the cabbage leaves out on the clingfilm, overlapping them slightly to form a sheet. Spread the shredded cabbage and shallots evenly on top, then roll up to form a sausage and wrap tightly in the clingfilm, twisting the ends to secure. Pierce the clingfilm with the tip of a knife to release any excess water, then chill the sausage for 2 hours.

To make the curry sauce, beat the egg yolks, curry powder, ½ teaspoon salt and the wine vinegar together in a bowl, then slowly whisk in the oil, drop by drop to begin with, then in a steady stream to make a smooth, thick mayonnaise. Stir in the apple juice until evenly combined, then taste and adjust the seasoning.

Heat your oven to 180°C. Heat your grill to its highest setting and oil a grill tray. Season the fish with salt and place skin side up on the grill tray.

Slice the cabbage roll carefully into four even lengths and remove the clingfilm. Place the cabbage rolls on a lined baking tray and warm through in the oven for 5 minutes or so.

Meanwhile, place the fish under the grill for 6 minutes or until just cooked. Gently warm the sauce in a pan until it just starts to steam, then take it off the heat and give it a good whisk.

When the fish is ready, spoon the sauce into warm deep plates. Add a cabbage roll and a fish fillet to each and finish with a drizzle of curry oil.

VEAL HOLSTEIN

Recipe by *TOM PARKER BOWLES*, food writer & critic, London, England

SERVINGS: 4 | **PREP TIME: 20 MINS** | **COOK TIME: 10 MINS** | **SKILL LEVEL: 1 (EASY)**

When I see this breadcrumb-clad beauty on the menu, little else matters. I couldn't care less if it's retro, or in or out of fashion. It's a northern European classic, simply schnitzel with added punch — topped with a fried egg, capers and anchovies. The Wolseley in London does a wonderful version, but I wish they wouldn't add the gravy. As for the veal, try to go for British rose veal. It doesn't have quite the same bland tenderness as the Continental milk-fed veal (in fact, it's almost a different product entirely), but as the calves are allowed space to move around and have a more natural, mixed diet, you can eat with conscience clear.

INGREDIENTS

25 g (1 oz) plain flour

a big pinch of mustard powder

6 large eggs

100 g fresh breadcrumbs

4 veal escalopes (about 150 g each), bashed between two pieces of clingfilm with a rolling pin until almost paper-thin

150 g unsalted butter

1 tbsp sunflower oil

2 heaped tbsp non-pareil capers, drained

2 tbsp finely chopped fresh parsley

juice of ½ lemon

8 anchovy fillets (the best you can find), drained

METHOD

Season the flour with the mustard powder, salt and pepper, and put it on a plate. Break two of the eggs into a shallow bowl and beat lightly. Put the breadcrumbs in another shallow bowl. Lightly season the veal, dip it in the seasoned flour, then the beaten egg, then the breadcrumbs.

Melt one-third of butter with the oil in a large, heavy-bottomed frying pan over a medium heat and cook the escalopes, two at a time, until golden — about 1½–2 minutes on each side. Remove and keep warm.

Wipe out the pan with a wad of kitchen paper, add half the remaining butter and fry the remaining eggs. Top each escalope with a runny-yolked fried egg.

Melt the remaining butter in the pan, add the capers and warm for a few seconds, then remove from the heat and add the parsley and a good squeeze of lemon.

Criss-cross each egg with two anchovy fillets, spoon over the capers and parsley and serve with French fries or sautéed potatoes.

SHAVED RAW BRUSSELS SPROUT SALAD WITH HAZELNUTS, POMEGRANATE & PUMPKIN SEEDS

Recipe by *LORRAINE PASCALE*, chef & TV presenter, London, England

SERVINGS: 4 | PREP TIME: 15–20 MINS | COOK TIME: 20 MINS | SKILL LEVEL: 1 (EASY)

There is only one thing which is not quite super-easy with this dish, and that is the cutting of the nutrient powerhouses that are brussels sprouts. I have recently dusted off my food processor and put one of those attachments on it that usually just stay on the top shelf of the cupboard. However, who would have thunk it but these attachments actually make the whole job so much easier and you can chop the whole lot in a few minutes! If, however, you do not have one of these machines, then put your favourite music on and enjoy slicing your sprouts.

INGREDIENTS

75 g pumpkin seeds

500 g brussels sprouts, outer leaves removed

100 g roasted hazelnuts, roughly chopped

1 x 400 g can Puy or green lentils, drained (or a 250 g pack of ready-to-eat Puy lentils)

75 g raisins

150 g pomegranate seeds (from 1 large pomegranate)

For the dressing

6 tbsp extra virgin olive oil

3 tbsp balsamic vinegar

DF, GF, V

METHOD

Put a medium frying pan on a medium–high heat and dry-fry the pumpkin seeds for 2–3 minutes until toasted and just beginning to pop. Remove and tip onto a small plate to cool.

Mix the dressing ingredients together in a really large bowl and season well with salt and pepper. Very thinly slice the sprouts by hand (or I like to use the slicing attachment on my food processor for a speedier job).

Toss the sprouts, pumpkin seeds, hazelnuts, lentils, raisins and all but a handful of pomegranate seeds into the dressing, giving it a good mix all together.

Spoon the salad out onto a large serving platter, sprinkle the remaining pomegranate seeds over the top and serve.

NEIL PERRY AM
CHEF & RESTAURATEUR

Being a restaurateur means I'm not always home for dinner with the family, so I love it when my girls come visit me after school and we share an early dinner together. This recipe is how we like to eat at home: very relaxed, informal and hands-on.

Neil

Sydney,
New South Wales

SPICY PRAWN TORTILLAS

Recipe by *NEIL PERRY* AM, chef & restaurateur, New South Wales, Australia

SERVINGS: 4 | **PREP TIME: 20 MINS PLUS MARINATING** | **SKILL LEVEL: 1 (EASY)**

INGREDIENTS

For the prawns

600 g green king prawns
3 cloves garlic, crushed
1 large Spanish onion,
  finely diced
1 tsp cumin seeds
1 tsp coriander seeds
2 tsp salsa macha
1 tsp sea salt
100 ml extra virgin olive oil
juice of 2 limes

For the salsa

5 Roma tomatoes
4 chipotles in adobo
  (see tip)

For the salad

2 cups shaved cabbage
2 cucumbers peeled,
  halved, de-seeded and
  cut into ½ cm semicircles
half a bunch of coriander
  leaves, washed and
  chopped

To serve

tortillas, enough to serve
  4 people

DF

METHOD

Peel and de-vein the prawns. In a bowl, mix the prawns with all the ingredients except the lime juice and leave to marinate for an hour.

Finely dice the tomatoes and finely mince the chipotles. Mix the salsa ingredients together with a sprinkle of sea salt and place in a small serving bowl.

Mix all the salad ingredients and place in a serving bowl.

To finish, heat a grill pan or pan to hot. Add the prawns and marinade, cook quickly on one side and toss to cook on the other. Don't overcook – it will happen quickly. Place the prawns in a serving bowl and squeeze the lime juice over. Heat the tortillas in a microwave.

Place all the dishes in the middle of the table, take a tortilla and spoon a bit of each dish on, roll and enjoy.

TIP

Salsa macha is a traditional chilli salsa from the Oaxacan and Veracruz regions of Mexico, made with extra virgin olive oil. It is available in specialty food stores, as are the chipotles in adobo, a spicy Mexican sauce (adobo) of smoke-dried jalapeños (chipotle).

BASIC FLAPJACKS

Recipe by *FRANCES QUINN*, baker & designer, Leicestershire, England

SERVINGS: 4 | **PREP TIME: 5 MINS** | **COOK TIME: 20 MINS** | **SKILL LEVEL: 1 (EASY)**

INGREDIENTS

50 g butter, roughly
   chopped
50 g golden caster sugar
1 tbsp golden syrup
100 g rolled oats

V

METHOD

You will need a 15 cm round, loose-bottomed tin, greased and base-lined.

Pre-heat the oven to 180°C/160°C fan.

Put the butter, sugar and golden syrup in a saucepan. Set it over a medium heat and warm, stirring occasionally, until the butter has melted and the sugar has dissolved. Take the saucepan off the heat and stir in the oats, combining everything thoroughly.

Transfer the mixture into the prepared tin and spread out evenly using the back of a spoon or spatula. Bake for 12–15 minutes or until golden-brown around the edges. Leave to cool in the tin.

TIPS

Although they are delicious on their own, flapjacks needn't be plain. I enjoy them coated with chocolate. In fact, this 15 cm round one can be made into something like a giant Chocolate Hobnob! Just cover it in 50 grams melted chocolate and use a palette knife to create biscuit markings on top.

I also love citrus zest in my flapjacks to give a really fruity flavour, and often substitute marmalade or honey for the golden syrup.

TAGLIATA DI MANZO

THINLY SLICED RARE PAN-FRIED BEEF WITH BALSAMIAC-DRESSED SALAD

Recipe by *THEO RANDALL*, Theo Randall at the InterContinental, London, England

SERVINGS: 4 | **PREP TIME: 5 MINS** | **COOK TIME: 5 MINS** | **SKILL LEVEL: 1 (EASY)**

This is a great way to serve a seared piece of fillet. The crusting of the thyme and sea salt on the outside gives it a lovely flavour and texture. Being such a simple dish, it is all about good ingredients — the tomatoes should be sweet and the Parmesan fresh. If you have some good balsamic vinegar, use it on this because it will work really well with the other ingredients.

INGREDIENTS

1 x 500 g piece of beef fillet (tail)

4 tbsp extra virgin olive oil

1 tsp chopped thyme

150 g datterini or cherry tomatoes, cut into quarters

100 g wild rocket

juice of ½ lemon

1 tsp aged balsamic vinegar

75 g Parmesan cheese shavings

GF

METHOD

Rub the fillet with 1 tablespoon of olive oil, then sprinkle over the thyme and season with salt and pepper.

Heat a heavy-based frying pan. Add the fillet and cook for 3–4 minutes, turning frequently to ensure an even searing that gives the meat a browned crust. Remove from the pan and leave to rest for 3 minutes.

Meanwhile, combine the tomatoes and rocket in a large bowl. Add the remaining olive oil and the lemon juice. Season to taste. Toss gently together, then spread the rocket and tomatoes on a large plate.

Thinly slice the beef and arrange on top of the rocket and tomatoes. Drizzle the balsamic vinegar over the beef and add a grinding of black pepper. Finish with the Parmesan shavings.

Franschhoek,
Western Cape

REUBEN RIFFEL
REUBEN'S

My past has a big impact on how I cook today. I love it when I get to see my kids' smiling faces as they tuck into bowls of hearty goodness, pretty much the same food that I used to enjoy as a child. What more can a parent ask for?

Reuben

PORK & BEANS

Recipe by *REUBEN RIFFEL*, Reuben's, Western Cape, South Africa

SERVINGS: 6 | PREP TIME: 10 MINS | COOK TIME: 2 HOURS PLUS RESTING | SKILL LEVEL: 1 (EASY)

INGREDIENTS

1 tbsp black peppercorns
2 bay leaves, dried
2 sprigs thyme
3 tbsp coarse salt
canola oil
2½ kg boneless pork belly

For the beans
olive oil
3 medium-sized red
  onions, coarsely chopped
3 cloves garlic, peeled
  and crushed
3 cups tomato passata
2 cups concentrated
  chicken stock
2 x 410g cans borlotti
  beans
2 x 410g cans red kidney
  beans
1 x 410g can white beans
dried origanum, to taste
smoked paprika, to taste
200 g Cheddar or
  mozzarella, cubed

GF

METHOD

Pre-heat the oven to 250°C. Crush together the black peppercorns, bay leaves and thyme with the coarse salt and a drizzle of canola oil. Using a sharp knife, score the skin of the pork belly. Rub the aromatics mixture all over the pork. Place in a roasting tray, fat side up, and roast for 15 minutes. Turn the oven temperature down to 170°C and roast for another 1 hour and 20 minutes.

Remove the meat from the oven and place another tray on top with enough weight to press down on the belly very lightly. Allow to cool like this for 2–3 hours. (This process is optional, but I like to have the fat side fairly flat and you also get rid of the excess fat.) Chop the cooled meat into cubes.

To cook the beans, add some olive oil to a wide pan and slowly sweat the onions and garlic in it without allowing them to brown. After about 4 minutes, add the passata and chicken stock, bring quickly to simmering point and then simmer slowly for 4 minutes. Add the beans, heat through, then add the cubed pork. Cook for 8 minutes. Add the origanum and smoked paprika, season to taste and just before you serve the dish, add the cubes of cheese and stir through. By the time you serve the cheese will be nicely melted.

272

DARREN ROBERTSON
THREE BLUE DUCKS

You really don't have to wait until dinner
for a great meal. Great coffee, eggs, butter,
avo, bread, a bit of salad... A fantastic
breakfast can be just as amazing as
anything consumed after dark.

Darren

Bronte,
New South Wales

AVOCADO, POACHED EGGS, SOURDOUGH, FERMENTED WHITE CABBAGE & FENNEL WITH SOME STUFF FROM THE GARDEN
AKA AVOCADO TOAST

Recipe by DARREN ROBERTSON, Three Blue Ducks, New South Wales, Australia

SERVINGS: 2 | PREP TIME: 10 MINS PLUS KRAUT PREPARATION | SKILL LEVEL: 2 (MODERATE)

INGREDIENTS

Fermented white cabbage and fennel, aka kraut

1 large white cabbage

1 bulb fennel

2 tbsp salt

4 tsp of your favourite spices, toasted (fennel, coriander, cumin or mustard seeds work a treat)

2 x 900 ml jars, sterilised

a handful of herbs and flowers from the garden – we like…
fennel fronds
parsley
basil
nasturtiums
pineapple sage
chamomile flowers
baby sorrel
chives

juice of 1 lime

1 tbsp good-quality olive oil

4 free-range eggs

1 sourdough bread roll, torn in half

1 clove garlic, halved

1 large, ripe avocado

1 tbsp fermented cabbage and fennel (see recipe above)

1 cornichon, chopped

DF, V

METHOD

The kraut recipe will fill a couple of jars, which is of course more than you're going to need for the poached eggs on toast. But if you're going to make your own kraut from scratch, it's well worth making a decent amount!

Remove the dark leaves from the cabbage, then core and shred. Core the fennel and slice it finely. Place the cabbage and fennel in a large bowl, then add the salt. Mix vigorously for 2 minutes and then set aside for 10 minutes to allow the water to leach out. Add the toasted spices, and give it another good mix. Taste the liquid. If it's super-salty, add a little water. If it's too bland, add a little more salt. Halve the mixture into each of the sterilised jars, ensuring there is enough liquid to cover the vegetables. Screw on the lid (not too tightly) and place the jars in a cool, dry place, away from direct sunlight, to ferment. Every 24 hours, gently loosen the lid to allow the gases to escape. Taste the kraut regularly, and once it's reached your preferred level of ferment-y goodness (anywhere from two days to a week), store it in the fridge until needed.

In a bowl, dress the leaves and flowers with a little lime juice, olive oil and salt and pepper to taste. Set aside.

To serve, heat a saucepan full of water to a low simmer. Add a little lime juice and gently crack the eggs in, one at a time. Poach the eggs for about 2 minutes, or until soft-poached. Heat a barbecue or chargrill and place on the bread, torn side down, until toasted. Place the toast on your favourite plate, rub it with the cut side of the garlic and set aside. Peel the avocado, remove the seed and slice the flesh. Season with salt and pepper and place on the toast. Top with some of the fermented vegetables, then two poached eggs, the chopped cornichons and a small pile of dressed herbs and flowers. Drizzle a little extra lime juice and olive oil on top, and a little pinch of salt and pepper.

ALMODROTE DE BERENJENA

EGGPLANT FLAN

Recipe by *CLAUDIA RODEN*, food writer, London, England

SERVINGS: 4–6 | **PREP TIME: 30 MINS** | **COOK TIME: 1¾ HOURS** | **SKILL LEVEL: 1 (EASY)**

This is one of the best-loved and most distinctive Jewish dishes of Turkey, the one everyone mentions as the favourite. A similar dish of mashed eggplant, eggs and cheese is mentioned in the records of the Court of the Inquisition in Spain as one that gave away Christian converts attached to their Jewish faith. The only similar dish I found is the papeton d'aubergines of Provence. Is there a link and a story? A mixture of feta and Kashkaval cheese is traditionally used, but other cheeses, like Cheddar and Gruyère, are also used (by Turkish Jews in England) with very pleasing effect.

INGREDIENTS

2 kg eggplant
2 large slices bread,
  crusts removed
150 g feta
6 eggs, lightly beaten
150 g grated kashkaval
  or Gruyère cheese
5 tbsp sunflower oil

V

METHOD

Pre-heat the oven to 180°C. Roast the eggplant for 45 minutes and allow to cool, then peel them. Put them in a colander and press with your hand to squeeze out as much of the juices as you can, then chop the flesh with two knives or, as is also the custom in Turkey, mash it with a wooden spoon. Do not use a food processor – that would change the texture.

Soak the bread in water until wet, then squeeze it dry. In a bowl, mash the feta with a fork. Add the eggs, bread, Kashkaval or Gruyère cheese (reserving 2–3 tablespoons) and 4 tablespoons of oil. Beat well. Add the eggplant and mix well. Pour the mixture into an oiled baking dish, sprinkle the top with 1 tablespoon of oil and the remaining grated cheese, and bake for 45 minutes to 1 hour, until lightly coloured.

NOTE

For almodrote de kalavasa, use boiled and chopped zucchini instead of eggplant.

RISOTTO CON PISELLI, LIMONE E RICOTTA

PEA, RICOTTA & LEMON ZEST RISOTTO

Recipe by *RUTH ROGERS*, The River Café, London, England

SERVINGS: 6 | **PREP TIME: 20 MINS** | **COOK TIME: 30 MINS** | **SKILL LEVEL: I (EASY)**

INGREDIENTS

1½ litres chicken stock

Maldon salt and freshly ground black pepper

3 kg fresh young peas (podded weight 1½ kg)

2 tbsp fresh mint leaves

3 cloves garlic, peeled, 2 chopped

200 g unsalted butter

500 g spring onions, roughly chopped

400 g Carnaroli or Arborio rice

2 tbsp torn fresh basil leaves

150 ml dry vermouth

250 g fresh ricotta cheese, lightly beaten

finely grated zest of 2 washed lemons

50 g Parmesan, freshly grated

GF

METHOD

Heat the chicken stock to boiling and check for seasoning. Bring a medium saucepan of water to the boil, and add ½ tablespoon salt, the peas, half the mint and the whole garlic clove. Simmer for 3–4 minutes or until the peas are al dente. Drain, keeping back 150 ml of the water. Return the peas, mint and garlic clove to this water and put aside.

Melt 150 grams of the butter in a large, thick-bottomed saucepan, add the spring onion and soften. Add the chopped garlic, then the rice, stirring for about 2–3 minutes to coat each grain. Add a ladle of hot stock and stir, adding another when the rice has absorbed the first. Continue stirring and adding stock for 10 minutes or until the rice is not quite al dente.

Add half the peas, keeping back the cooked garlic and mint and their liquor. Mash together the remainder of the peas, mint and garlic with the liquor in a food processor, then add to the risotto and stir. Stir in the basil. Add the vermouth, about 2 tablespoons of the ricotta, and the remaining butter. Cook briefly to wilt the basil and melt the butter. Test for doneness: the rice should be al dente.

Serve with the remaining ricotta over each portion, sprinkled with lemon zest, salt, pepper and Parmesan.

SPANAKOPITA SPIRALS

Recipe by *VONNI ROMANO*, Maria's Greek Café & Restaurant, Western Cape, South Africa

SERVINGS: 6 | PREP TIME: 40 MINS | COOK TIME: 20 MINS | SKILL LEVEL: 1 (EASY)

INGREDIENTS

125 g phyllo pastry, thawed

olive oil, for brushing

For the filling

30 ml olive oil

1 medium onion, finely chopped

a generous grating of nutmeg

1 small bunch spring onions, finely chopped

200 g Swiss chard

500 g baby spinach, well rinsed

200 g feta, crumbled

30 ml snipped fresh flat-leaf parsley

30 ml snipped fresh mint

30 ml snipped fresh dill

2 medium-sized eggs, beaten

V

METHOD

To make the filling, heat 30 ml oil and cook onion and nutmeg for a few minutes until soft. Add spring onion and cook for a minute. Chop Swiss chard coarsely and add to the onion. Stir-fry briefly until just wilted. Add baby spinach and cook for a minute. Remove pan from the heat and allow to cool before adding the feta, snipped herbs, eggs, and some salt and ground black pepper. Mix well and check seasoning. Cover and store in the fridge until needed.

Pre-heat the oven to 180°C. Remove the phyllo pastry from its packaging, and cover with a dry cloth. Place a damp cloth on top of this to prevent the pastry from drying out. Taking one sheet at a time, brush lightly with oil and fold in half, brushing with oil again.

Spread a line of filling lengthwise along the bottom. Roll up loosely into a sausage shape. Fold into a spiral and place, cut-side down, on a greased oven tray. Brush the tops and sides with oil and bake in the centre of the oven for 15–20 minutes or until crisp and golden-brown.

TIP

The wonderful taste of these spinach and feta spirals depends entirely on really fresh garden herbs. No matter how small my home may be, I always make sure that I have the pleasure of picking my own on demand.

MICHEL ROUX
THE WATERSIDE INN

All of us do have a philosophy about food one way or another. Mine is very simple – it's all about the main ingredient. I don't want to muck it up, I want to extract the best flavour of what I'm going to cook. Don't kill the best ingredient you've got a second time!

Bray,
Berkshire

TARTE FINE AU CITRON
LEMON TART

Recipe by *MICHEL ROUX*, The Waterside Inn, Berkshire, England

SERVINGS: 8 | **PREP TIME: 40 MINS PLUS CHILLING** | **COOK TIME: 1⅓ HOURS** | **SKILL LEVEL: 2 (MODERATE)**

INGREDIENTS

For the pâté sablée
(use 350 g)
250 g plain flour
200 g butter, cut into
  small pieces and slightly
  softened
100 g icing sugar, sifted
pinch of salt
2 egg yolks
butter, to grease

For the filling
5 eggs
180 g caster sugar
150 ml double cream
finely grated zest and
  strained juice of 2 lemons
1 egg yolk mixed with
  1 tsp milk, to glaze

V

METHOD

To make the pâté sablée, heap the flour on the work surface and make a well. Put in the butter, icing sugar and salt. With your fingertips, mix and cream the butter with the sugar and salt, then add the egg yolks and work them in delicately.

Little by little, draw the flour into the centre and work the mixture delicately with your fingers until you have a homogeneous dough.

Using the palm of your hand, push the dough away from you three or four times until it is completely smooth. Roll it into a ball, wrap in cling film and refrigerate until ready to use. It will keep in the fridge for up to a week, or in the freezer for up to three weeks. This makes about 650 grams, but you'll only need 350 grams.

Lightly butter a 22 cm tart tin, about 2 cm deep, and chill on a baking tray. Roll out the pastry to a round, 3–4 mm thick. Drape it over the rolling pin and unfurl over the tart tin. Line the tin with the pastry, gently tapping it in with a knob of pastry. Trim off the excess pastry around the rim then, using your index finger and thumb, gently press the pastry edges up the sides of the tin to form a fluted lip, about 2 mm. Refrigerate for 20 minutes.

Pre-heat the oven to 190°C. For the filling, lightly whisk the eggs and sugar in a bowl, without letting the mixture turn pale. In another, chilled, bowl, whisk the cream for a few seconds, then mix it into the eggs. Add the lemon zest and juice, stir briefly, cover with cling film and refrigerate.

Line the chilled pastry case with greaseproof paper, fill with baking beans and bake blind for 15 minutes. Remove the beans and paper, leave for a couple of minutes, then brush the base and sides of the pastry with the egg glaze. Bake for a further 5 minutes, until lightly coloured. Take out and lower the temperature to 150°C.

Lightly whisk the chilled lemon filling, then pour it into the tart case up to the level of the lip. Immediately bake for about 1 hour, until lightly set. Leave for about 5 minutes, then carefully remove the tart from the tin. Leave to cool on a wire rack for at least 4 hours before serving.

Serve the tart as it is, or sprinkled with a generous layer of icing sugar. It is delicious accompanied by red berries in season.

SID SAHRAWAT
SIDART & CASSIA

While being a chef is extremely rewarding, I don't see my daughter Zoya as much as I'd like to as I work such long hours at the restaurants. When I have a day off, one of the things we love to do together is to go foraging for herbs. Foraging suggests we go into the wild but we just pick herbs from our surroundings; I love that we can have that connection with nature together.

Sid

Ponsonby,
Auckland

BUTTER DUCK

Recipes by *SID SAHRAWAT*, Sidart & Cassia, Auckland, New Zealand

SERVINGS: 4–6 | PREP TIME: 10 MINS PLUS CHILLING | COOK TIME: 1½ HOURS | SKILL LEVEL: 2 (MODERATE)

INGREDIENTS

6 cloves garlic, finely grated
4 tsp finely grated, peeled fresh ginger
4 tsp ground turmeric
2 tsp garam masala
2 tsp ground coriander
2 tsp ground cumin
1½ cups whole-milk yoghurt (not Greek)
1 tbsp kosher salt

2 tbsp tandoori masala paste
1 whole duck
3 tbsp ghee or vegetable oil
1 small onion, thinly sliced
¼ cup tomato paste
6 cardamom pods, crushed
2 dried chillies or ½ tsp crushed
  red chilli flakes

1 x 400 g can whole tomatoes
2 cups cream
¾ cup chopped fresh coriander,
  plus sprigs for garnish
steamed basmati rice, for serving

GF

METHOD

Combine garlic, ginger, turmeric, garam masala, coriander and cumin in a small bowl. Whisk yoghurt, salt and half of the spice mixture in a medium-sized bowl with the tandoori paste; rub all over duck and turn to coat. Cover and chill for 4–6 hours. Cover and chill remaining spice mixture.

Heat ghee or oil in a large heavy pot over medium heat. Add onion, tomato paste, cardamom and chillies, and cook, stirring often, until tomato paste has darkened and onion is soft, about 5 minutes. Add remaining half of spice mixture and cook, stirring often, until bottom of pot begins to brown, about 4 minutes.

Add tomatoes with juice, crushing them with your hands as you add them. Bring to a boil, reduce heat and simmer, stirring often and scraping up browned bits from the bottom of the pot, until sauce thickens, 8–10 minutes.

Add cream and coriander. Simmer, stirring occasionally, until sauce thickens, 30–40 minutes.

Meanwhile, pre-heat the oven to 200°C. Line a rimmed baking sheet with foil and set a wire rack on top of sheet. Arrange duck on rack, skin-side up. Cook until duck starts to blacken in spots (it will not be cooked through), about 20 minutes. Reduce oven temperature to 180°C and cook for a further 40 minutes.

Portion duck into even pieces, add to sauce, and simmer, stirring occasionally, until duck is cooked through, 8–10 minutes. Serve with rice and coriander sprigs.

TIP

The duck can be roasted a day ahead. Cover, chill, then reheat before serving. Spices can be found in any Indian grocery store.

BEETROOT RAITA

SERVINGS: 4 | PREP TIME: 5 MINS | SKILL LEVEL: 1 (EASY)

INGREDIENTS

2 medium-sized beetroots
3 cups thick yoghurt
1 tsp roasted cumin powder
1 tsp red chilli powder
fresh mint leaves, for garnish

GF, V

METHOD

Peel skin off beetroots. Grate beetroots using a box grater or food processor.

Whisk yoghurt in a bowl. Add beetroot, cumin, chilli and salt to taste and mix well. Garnish with mint leaves and serve.

Note: The bright, dark colour of the beetroot will bleed and change the colour of the yoghurt to dark pink.

PANEER TIKKA

SERVINGS: 4 | **PREP TIME: 10 MINS PLUS MARINATING** | **COOK TIME: 15 MINS** | **SKILL LEVEL: 2 (MODERATE)**

INGREDIENTS

For the marinade
½ tsp lemon juice
½ tsp chilli powder
½ tsp roasted and ground cumin seeds
¾ cup fresh yoghurt
½ tbsp crushed ginger paste
½ tsp green chilli paste
1 tsp ground black pepper

½ tsp carom seeds
1 tsp ground fennel seeds
¾ tsp ground turmeric
½ tbsp ground paprika
⅓ cup besan (Bengal gram flour)
1 tsp oil
salt to taste
a few saffron strands, dissolved in
    1 tbsp milk

For the tikka
12 x 5 cm cubes paneer
1 tbsp oil, for cooking
1 tsp chaat masala
1 tbsp finely chopped fresh coriander

GF, V

METHOD

Combine paneer and marinade in a bowl, toss gently and set aside to marinate for at least half an hour. Soak four wooden satay sticks in water. On each satay stick, arrange three pieces of paneer. Repeat with the remaining ingredients to make three more tikkas.

Heat a non-stick frying pan or griddle, and cook the tikkas on a medium flame, basting with oil, until the paneer is light brown in colour on all sides. Alternatively, grill the paneer tikkas on a tandoor or barbecue grill until light brown in colour on all sides. Serve immediately, sprinkled with chaat masala and coriander.

TIP

Chaat masala can be found in any Indian grocery store, as can the other spices, as well as besan and paneer. If paneer is bought frozen, thaw before marinating.

CHICKPEA KEBABS

SERVINGS: 4 | **PREP TIME: 10 MINS** | **COOK TIME: 20 MINS** | **SKILL LEVEL: 2 (MODERATE)**

INGREDIENTS

1 x 400 g can chickpeas
1 medium-sized onion
1 fresh green chilli
1 tbsp chopped fresh mint
1 tbsp chopped fresh
    coriander leaves
1 tsp coriander powder
½ tsp red chilli powder
½ tbsp ginger paste
½ tsp garam masala
2 tbsp chickpea flour
oil, for frying
fresh mint leaves,
    for garnish

DF, GF, V

METHOD

Drain and rinse chickpeas and place in a large bowl. Mash with a wooden spoon, a blender or with your hands, making a semi-coarse mixture which is not too smooth.

Finely chop onion and chilli, and add to chickpeas with the rest of the ingredients. Mix well. Form into small, round-shaped kebabs or patties.

Shallow-fry the kebabs in medium–hot oil until crisp and browned on both sides. Garnish with mint leaves and serve hot.

TIP

Fry one kebab to check that it holds together. If the mixture is too wet and breaks, add more chickpea flour.

'NDUJA BRUSCHETTA

Recipe by *NIGEL SLATER*, food writer & TV broadcaster, London, England

SERVINGS: 1 | PREP TIME: 5 MINS | COOK TIME: 5 MINS | SKILL LEVEL: 1 (EASY)

INGREDIENTS

Per sandwich

1 thick slice sourdough
  or ciabatta
olive oil
85 g (3 oz) 'nduja (a spicy,
  spreadable salami)
50 g (1½ oz) soft goat's
  curd or cheese
3 sprigs thyme
4–6 black olives

METHOD

Toast the bread lightly on both sides. Leave the grill on.

Trickle enough olive oil over one side of the toast to thoroughly moisten it. Place a slice of 'nduja on the bread, add the goat's curd, thyme leaves and a little trickle of oil, then slide under the grill for a few minutes till the 'nduja is warm. Add the olives, trickle over a little more olive oil and eat immediately.

CHARMAINE SOLOMON'S TRADITIONAL CHRISTMAS CAKE

Recipe by *CHARMAINE SOLOMON OAM*, cook & author, New South Wales, Australia

MAKES: 1 CAKE | **PREP TIME: 3 HOURS (APPROX.)** | **COOK TIME: 2¼–2½ HOURS** | **SKILL LEVEL: 2 (MODERATE)**

INGREDIENTS

For the cake

250 g raisins, chopped

385 g sultanas, chopped

250 g mixed glacé fruit such as pineapple, apricot and quince, (avoid using fig), chopped

260 g preserved ginger, chopped

500 g chow chow preserves

120 g mixed peel, chopped

260 g glacé cherries, halved

260 g raw cashews or blanched almonds, finely chopped

125 ml brandy

375 g butter

500 g caster sugar

12 egg yolks (reserve 6 egg whites for this recipe)

2 tsp lemon zest, finely grated

1 ½ tsp ground cardamom

1 tsp ground cinnamon

1 tsp nutmeg, freshly grated

¾ tsp ground cloves

2 tbsp natural vanilla extract

1 tbsp natural almond extract

2 tbsp rose water, or to taste

1 tbsp honey

250 g fine semolina

6 egg whites

1 quantity almond paste (see right), for icing (optional)

For the almond paste

250 g ground almonds

500 g icing sugar, sifted

1 small egg, beaten

1 tbsp brandy

1 tbsp sherry

½ tsp natural almond extract (optional)

1 egg white, beaten, for brushing

GF, V

METHOD

Line a 25 cm round or square cake tin with three layers of brown paper, then one layer of baking paper liberally brushed with melted butter. To insulate the tin even more, wrap the outside with a sheet of newspaper folded into three and secure it with kitchen string.

Combine the raisins, sultanas, mixed glacé fruit, preserved ginger, chow chow preserves, mixed peel, glacé cherries and cashews in a large bowl. Pour over the brandy, cover, and set aside. (This step can be done the day before, allowing the fruit more time to soak in the brandy, if desired.)

Preheat the oven to 130°C. Cream together the butter and sugar until light and fluffy. Add the egg yolks, one at a time, beating well after each addition. Add the lemon zest, spices, vanilla and almond extracts, rose water and honey and mix well. Add the semolina and beat until well combined.

Transfer the mixture to a large bowl or pan and use your hands to mix in the fruit until thoroughly combined – it's much easier than a spoon and professional pastry cooks do it this way.

In a separate bowl, beat the egg whites until stiff peaks form, then fold through the fruit mixture until just combined. Pour into the prepared cake tin and bake in the oven for 2¼–2½ hours, covering the cake with foil after the first hour to prevent over-browning. The cake will be very rich and moist when done. If you prefer a darker and drier result, bake for 4½–5 hours – it will not be dry, but certainly firmer than if you cook for a shorter time. Allow to cool completely, preferably overnight, then remove the paper and wrap the cake in foil. A tablespoon or two of brandy may be sprinkled over the cake just before wrapping. If desired, ice the cake with the almond paste. This cake can be stored in an airtight container for one year or longer.

Mix together the ground almonds and icing sugar in a large bowl, add the combined egg, brandy, sherry and almond extract, if using, then knead until the mixture holds together. Roll out half the almond paste on a work surface dusted with icing sugar and cut to fit the top of the cake. Brush the traditional Christmas cake with egg white, then place the almond paste on top and press lightly with a rolling pin. Roll the remaining almond paste into a strip to fit around the side of the cake.

RICK STEIN'S SHRIMP & DILL FRITTERS WITH OUZO

Recipe by *RICK STEIN OBE*, chef, food writer & TV presenter, Cornwall, England

SERVINGS: 4–8 | **PREP TIME: 20 MINS** | **COOK TIME: 15 MINS** | **SKILL LEVEL: 1 (EASY)**

This comes from a tiny fishing village called Gerakas, 40 minutes north of Monemvasia in the Peloponnese. The drive is spectacular, and Gerakas itself is the Greek fishing village by which all others must be judged. This was designed to use the tiny shrimps in the inlet on which Gerakas lies. I particularly enjoy the subtle flavours of dill and ouzo.

INGREDIENTS

175 g plain flour

½ tsp baking powder

½ tsp salt

300 ml water

1 tbsp ouzo (or pastis)

300 g whole raw Falmouth Bay shrimps or brown shrimps, or 175 g raw, peeled prawns cut into slices 5 mm thick

2 spring onions, very finely sliced

1 tbsp chopped dill

olive oil, for shallow-frying

DF

METHOD

Into a large bowl, sift the flour and baking powder, add the salt, then make a well in the centre and add the water and ouzo or pastis. Gradually incorporate the flour into the liquid to make a thick batter. Fold in the shrimps/prawns, spring onions and dill.

Pour olive oil to a depth of about 5 mm into a frying pan and place over a high heat. When hot, carefully add large spoonfuls of batter into the pan and spread out a little with the back of a spoon so they develop thin, crispy edges. Cook 2–3 at a time, turn over after 2 minutes and repeat until puffed up and golden on both sides.

Remove from the pan and drain on kitchen paper. Serve immediately.

FLEUR SULLIVAN
FLEURS PLACE

When I first opened Fleurs Place, I would have people sitting at tables, cutlery in hands and I would have to say – see the boat coming around the corner, it's got your fish on it!

Every day, from the moment I open my eyes, I look down into the bay – what's the water like, where are the fishermen, are the boats out, will I get any fish today? Each day, when the restaurant fills with people from all over the world, I am reminded how fortunate I am. Every day is a highlight for me. I am on people's bucket lists now and I think that's pretty amazing!

Fleur

*Moeraki,
Otago*

SEAFOOD CHOWDER

Recipe by *FLEUR SULLIVAN*, Fleurs Place, Otago, New Zealand

SERVINGS: 8–10 | **PREP TIME: 10 MINS** | **COOK TIME: 15 MINS** | **SKILL LEVEL: 1–2 (EASY–MODERATE)**

INGREDIENTS

200 g butter

1 onion, diced

2 carrots, diced

2 sticks celery, diced

200 g plain flour

100 ml white wine

150 g tomato paste

2 litres fish stock, warmed

1 tsp fennel seeds, ground

1 tsp smoked ground
 paprika

2 bay leaves

1 tsp chopped fresh thyme

500 g fish, diced

20 mussels, de-bearded
 and washed

30 littleneck clams,
 washed

20 queen scallops,
 washed

METHOD

In a large heavy-bottomed pot, melt butter and add diced vegetables. Sweat for a couple of minutes but do not allow to colour. Add flour and cook for a further 2 minutes or until mixture has a sandy texture.

Slowly pour in the wine and tomato paste, and bring together as it thickens to remove all the lumps.

Add the warmed fish stock slowly, stirring continuously, and drop in the spices and herbs. Allow all this to come to the boil, taking care not to let it catch the bottom of the pan.

Add all the fish and shellfish, and simmer until the shells begin to open (only 2–3 minutes) and the fish is cooked through. Discard any shellfish that doesn't open.

TIPS

Making your own stock is the key to an adventurous and infectious journey into creating naturally good food.

'Prep time' depends on whether you gather your ingredients from the wild and your garden or from the supermarket!

SARAH SWAN & JEREMY BURN
100 MILE TABLE

It's a nice little bit of rebellion, making bacon-and-egg butties around here.
Byron Bay is a wonderful town of hippies and chia seeds and gluten-free
organics and that's important. But we like bacon. And eggs. And organic
food. And chia seeds. We just don't do so many.

Sarah & Jeremy

Byron Bay,
New South Wales

GRANOLA

Recipes by *SARAH SWAN & JEREMY BURN*, 100 Mile Table, New South Wales, Australia

MAKES: ½ KG (APPROX.) | **PREP TIME: 5 MINS** | **COOK TIME: 25–35 MINS** | **SKILL LEVEL: 2 (MODERATE)**

INGREDIENTS

2½ tbsp coconut oil

½ cup real maple syrup

3 tbsp honey

1 tsp vanilla essence

350 g rolled oats

60 g sunflower seeds

60 g pumpkin seeds

30 g sesame seeds

60 g shredded coconut

300 g dried blueberries

400 g dried pears, sliced thinly

V

METHOD

Pre-heat the oven to 160°C.

Add the coconut oil, maple syrup, honey and vanilla to a large mixing bowl and mix well. Add the oats and seeds and mix well to combine.

Transfer the granola mix to a baking tray and place in the oven. Cook until golden, (about 20–30 minutes) stirring well every 5 minutes or so because it will cook faster around the edges than on the inside.

When just golden, add the coconut and return to the oven for a final 5 minutes.

Remove the granola from the oven and mix the blueberries and sliced pear through.

When cool, store in airtight jars. Serve with your favourite milk, yoghurt and fresh seasonal fruit or fruit compote.

BACON & EGG BUTTY

SERVINGS: 4 | **PREP TIME: 15–20 MINS** | **SKILL LEVEL: 1 (EASY)**

INGREDIENTS

4 medium-sized rolls (we like corn rolls)

4 rashers organic bacon, rind removed

4 whole organic eggs

4 tbsp tomato relish or good-quality chutney

4 tbsp Green Goddess dressing

For the Green Goddess dressing (makes 1½ cups)

1 cup mayonnaise

½ cup sour cream

juice of 1 lemon

1 small clove garlic

1 cup herb leaves, finely chopped (we use parsley and tarragon with a little sage, oregano and marjoram)

3 tbsp finely chopped chives

METHOD

Slice the rolls in half, and toast – we toast on the cut side only, then warm the tops and bottoms with the roof of the sandwich press, but you can do this however you want. Let's face it, it's not rocket science. If you are making this for breakfast at home, I would do the whole lot on the barbecue.

Meanwhile, pop your bacon rashers on to cook, followed closely by the eggs. I like to break the yolks with a single stab from a fork and then keep the eggs contained by 'rounding them up' to get an even egg that isn't going to run out as soon as you bite into it. That said, do remove the egg before it goes hard.

To make the Green Goddess dressing, mix the mayonnaise and sour cream together until smooth. Add the lemon juice and whisk to combine. Finely crush the garlic and add with all the chopped herbs, then season with sea salt and freshly ground pepper to taste. Keeps covered in the fridge for up to three days.

Spread the tomato relish or chutney over the toasted bottoms of the four rolls and spread Green Goddess over the tops. Place an egg on top of the relish, followed by the bacon, with each rasher curled into a roll. Add the top half to each roll and serve.

PABLO TORDESILLAS
CHEF & RESTAURATEUR

There are a lot of similarities between the Spanish and Australian style of living. In particular, we love getting together with friends and family when the weather's good and barbecuing the hell out of everything! It really does give a flavour to food that nothing else can.

Pablo

Coorparoo, Queensland

OCTOPUS A LA PARRILLA &
RUNNER BEAN SALAD
BARBECUED OCTOPUS SALAD

Recipe by *PABLO TORDESILLAS*, chef & restaurateur, Queensland, Australia

SERVINGS: 6 | PREP & COOK TIME: 1¼ HOURS | SKILL LEVEL: 1 (EASY)

INGREDIENTS

100 g salt
1 bay leaf
1 wine cork (required
 by tradition!)
1 kg octopus, cleaned
3 large-bulb spring onions
2 cloves garlic, peeled
750 g runner beans
⅓ bunch flat-leaf parsley
400 g Kipfler potatoes
140 ml extra virgin olive
 oil
1 tbsp sweet Spanish
 paprika (pimentón)
150 g black olives
lemon juice to taste

DF, GF

METHOD

Start your coals or wood fire (you could also use a gas barbecue).

Three-quarters fill a large pot with water and add salt, bay leaf and wine cork. Bring to the boil and dip the octopus in for about 10 seconds to set its gelatine. Bring the water back up to the boil and re-dip the octopus. Repeat twice more, leaving the octopus in the last time. Turn the heat down and simmer for 40–45 minutes. Use a skewer to check the top part of the tentacles – if it's ready, the skewer should go through without much resistance. Leave to cool in the cooking liquor.

In the meantime, prepare your ingredients. Finely chop the spring onions and garlic. Top and tail the runner beans and cut at an angle into short lengths. Wash the parsley and chop roughly. Wash the potatoes, boil for 6–8 minutes depending on size, and cut into 5 mm rounds. If you wish, you can use the octopus liquid for cooking the potatoes.

Heat 100 ml of the olive oil in a medium-sized, heavy-based pan over a low flame, then add the onion and garlic and sweat gently for about 20 minutes, stirring occasionally to avoid browning. Once they're soft, remove from the heat and add the paprika. Keep stirring so it doesn't burn.

Blanch the runner beans in salted boiling water, then drain and, while they're still hot, incorporate with the onion and garlic mixture along with the potatoes and black olives. The residual heat from the beans will help to blend all the ingredients together.

Once the coals are ready, chargrill the octopus until the ends of the tentacles are charred, crisp and smoky; this takes about 3–4 minutes each side. Cut the octopus into chunks, keeping the tentacle ends in one piece, and toss into the bean mixture. Adjust seasoning with salt and pepper, dress with lemon juice and remaining olive oil, sprinkle the parsley over and mix lightly.

ZUCCHINI SOUP WITH CHARD BRUSCHETTA

Recipe by *VALENTINE WARNER*, chef, food writer & TV presenter, London, England

SERVINGS: 6 | PREP TIME: 30 MINS | COOK TIME: 55 MINS | SKILL LEVEL: I (EASY)

INGREDIENTS

3 tbsp olive oil

1 medium-sized onion, finely chopped

7–9 medium-sized zucchinis (about 1 kg), cut into 1½ cm slices

3 cloves garlic, peeled

good grating of nutmeg

a small sprig of rosemary

30 g Parmesan rind, if you have some handy

550 ml whole milk

1 tsp flaked sea salt

For the chard bruschetta

4–5 big Swiss chard leaves

extra virgin olive oil, for splashing

a squeeze of lemon juice

6 thin slices of rustic bread or ciabatta

1 good large clove garlic, peeled

To serve

Parmesan cheese

a little extra virgin olive oil

METHOD

To make the soup, pour the olive oil into a large, heavy pan and in it soften the onion over a medium heat for 8 minutes or so, stirring occasionally. Add the zucchini with the garlic, nutmeg, a good grinding of black pepper, rosemary and Parmesan rind (this will give depth to the soup in the absence of stock). Mix everything together before covering with a lid and leaving to cook for a further 20–25 minutes, stirring occasionally. After this time the zucchini should be very soft while retaining a pleasant green colour. Pick out the rosemary stalk, which will have dropped its leaves.

While the zucchini sweats it out, start making the bruschetta. Put a pan of salted water on to boil. Rip up the chard leaves and boil them for 5 minutes or so until tender. Drain the chard thoroughly and chop it very finely while it is still hot. Put it in a bowl with a generous splash of extra virgin olive oil, some salt and a light squeeze of lemon juice – just enough to give it a little edge. Leave the chard to one side. Pre-heat the grill to its highest setting.

To finish the soup, add the milk to the zucchini and gently simmer for 10 minutes or so without the lid. Do not let the soup boil. Take out the Parmesan rind and purée the soup in a food processor or with a stick blender until very smooth. Return it to the pan and place it over a very low heat to keep it hot. Season with the salt – probably a little more than you would normally use. Add a little more milk if you feel the soup is too thick.

To serve, top with grated Parmesan and a splash of olive oil.

MATT WILKINSON
MR WILKINSON'S

Someone asked me recently, "What makes having a family so special?" I think it's one of those things you don't really know how special it is until you have one of your own. Once you do, there's something amazing that happens which brings you together. I think one of the best things about having a family is the coming together and sharing of food. The food can be simple, but it's the people around you that create the memory, not just the food itself.

Northcote, Victoria

I HATE PESTO

Recipe by *MATT WILKINSON*, Mr Wilkinson's, Victoria, Australia

SERVINGS: 500 ML (APPROX.) | **PREP TIME: 5 MINS** | **SKILL LEVEL: I (EASY)**

When I was growing up, my dad used to make us pasta with pesto from a jar and I hated it! These days, we grow basil in huge amounts at home and my kids absolutely love it.

INGREDIENTS

2 big handfuls basil
  leaves, washed

1 tbsp toasted pine nuts,
  plus extra untoasted
  pine nuts for garnishing

2 tbsp finely grated
  Parmesan, with extra
  for garnishing

juice of ½ lemon

½ cup olive oil

METHOD

This is the basic pesto recipe we use – put it all in the blender, season with salt and pepper, and blitz until smooth but with a few small chunks. Garnish with the extra pine nuts and Parmesan.

TIPS

The pasta we serve with this does not resemble anything like the penne from my childhood years. I love different types of pasta shapes – seriously, an extra few dollars for a good dried pasta and some different shapes makes all the difference and is fun for the kids. I have provided a list below of some of the different shapes we like with pesto:

- bucatini (like a thicker spaghetti, but hollow)

- matriciani (similar to bucatini but folded over rather than a tube)

- trofie (torpedo-shaped spirals)

- spaghettoni (extra-long spaghetti)

- orecchiette (little ears)

- trecce dell'orto ('braids of the garden'; tight twists in five colours)

See the cooking instructions on the packet – I generally have no idea!

SAUSAGE ROLLS WITH TOMATO RELISH

Recipe by *DANIEL WILSON*, Huxtable, Victoria, Australia

MAKES: ABOUT 50 | PREP TIME: 1 HOUR PLUS FREEZING | COOK TIME: 20 MINS | SKILL LEVEL: 2 (MODERATE)

INGREDIENTS

400 g beef mince
200 g veal mince
200 g pork mince
1 medium carrot, minced
½ stick celery, minced
1 brown onion, minced
¼ cup finely
   chopped parsley
2 cloves garlic, minced
2 tbsp potato starch
   (available at Asian
   grocery stores)
8 sheets butter puff pastry
4 egg yolks,
   mixed with a fork

For the tomato relish
4 ripe tomatoes, diced
2 brown onions, diced
6 cloves garlic, sliced
½ cup raw sugar
½ cup malt vinegar
½ cup water
1 stick cinnamon
2 star anise

METHOD

For the sausage mix: place all three meats in a food processor and pulse until almost fine, but with some texture still. Place in a large bowl and add the vegetables, parsley, garlic, potato starch, and salt and pepper to taste. Mix well, until the sausage mix is emulsified. You can do this by beating it against the sides of the bowl. You must make sure that it remains as cold as possible at all times, otherwise it can split. Reserve, covered, in the fridge until needed.

To make the sausage rolls: place a sheet of puff pastry on your chopping board and cut it in half lengthways. Try to work quickly so that the pastry doesn't get too warm and soft. Roll enough of the sausage mix into a 2 cm thick log to fit the length of the pastry. Place on the pastry, about a third of the way back from one edge. Using a pastry brush, place some egg yolk on the wide part of the pastry. Fold over the narrow part of the pastry and stick it down on the part with the egg. Try to make sure that the pastry is snug around the sausage, then press the two layers of pastry together with a fork all the way along the joined pastry. Place on a lined tray in the freezer to firm up (freezing the sausage rolls makes them much easier to cut, and also the pastry cooks better from frozen). Repeat with the rest of the pastry and sausage mix.

For the relish: cook everything down together until thick. Remove spices, and blitz in a food processor.

To cook the sausage rolls: pre-heat the oven to 200°C. Remove the sausage roll logs from the freezer, brush the tops with egg yolk and allow them to sit for 10–15 minutes to soften slightly. Slice into about eitgh pieces per log, or whatever size you like. Place on a lined tray, without overcrowding them. Place in the oven for 20 minutes. The sausage rolls should be golden and the pastry crisp. Allow to sit for 5 minutes before serving, as they will be very hot!

Alternative 'grown-up' version: dice 150 grams sharp-tasting Cheddar and 3 tablespoons of pickled jalapeños and mix into the sausage mix!

ALLA WOLF-TASKER AM
LAKE HOUSE

———

It wasn't beautiful here in the beginning, it was a paddock on a swamp. I was a very young woman, returned from France, intent on creating in Australia something of what I had seen. Now, we're into our fourth decade. People ask me if I feel we've succeeded. Well, I think we've probably well and truly exceeded expectations.

Alla

Daylesford, Victoria

THE BEETROOT HARVEST

Recipe by *ALLA WOLF-TASKER AM*, Lake House, Victoria, Australia

SERVINGS: 2–4 | **PREP TIME: 1 HOUR** | **COOK TIME: 30–40 MINS** | **SKILL LEVEL: 2 (MODERATE)**

INGREDIENTS

For the baby beetroots

8 baby beetroots
  (may be different
  colours)

½ cup sugar

1 tbsp red wine vinegar

For the beetroot remoulade

2 medium-sized beetroots

150 ml good homemade
  mayonnaise

1 tsp Dijon mustard

2 shallots, diced finely

1 tsp lilliput (tiny) capers,
  washed and drained

1 medium-sized crunchy
  dill cucumber, diced
  finely

For the roasted beetroots

1 medium-sized beetroot

olive oil, to dress

Chioggia carpaccio

1 medium-sized chioggia
  beetroot

Garnish

seasonal herbs and
  edible flowers

DF, GF, V

METHOD

Baby beetroots: wash baby beetroots, leaving 2 cm of stem on. If still intact, scrub but do not trim off the roots. Place all ingredients in a pot along with enough water to cover – if using different-coloured beetroots, you will need to cook them separately. Cover with a circle of greaseproof paper, and simmer till cooked; about 15 minutes. Cool beetroots, then cut off stems. Peel beetroots, including the roots.

Beetroot remoulade: pre-heat oven to 165°C. Wrap beetroots in tinfoil and roast for about 30–40 minutes or until easily pierced with a knife. (Roast your other beetroots – see below – at the same time.) Cool until easy to handle, then peel and julienne. Mix mayonnaise and mustard to make remoulade dressing, then combine all remaining ingredients, including julienned beetroot. Add salt and pepper to taste.

Roasted beetroots: scrub beetroots, wrap in tinfoil and roast at 165°C until easily pierced with a knife; about 30–40 minutes. Cool, peel and dice. Toss with a little olive oil, salt and freshly ground pepper.

Chioggia carpaccio: scrub and peel raw chioggia beetroot. (Chioggia is an interesting heirloom variety that has 'bull's-eye' markings. You can also use normal beetroot.) Slice beetroots paper-thin, using a mandolin. Dress with a little olive oil, salt and freshly ground pepper.

Assembly: on a rectangular plate, place an arrangement of diced roast edbeetroots, whole baby beetroots (halve if large) and spoonfuls of beetroot remoulade. Intersperse with quarter- and half-slices of raw chioggia. Garnish with herbs and flowers.

ZUCCHINI NOODLES WITH AVOCADO PESTO

Recipe by *ELLA WOODWARD,* food writer & blogger, London, England

SERVINGS: 4 | **PREP TIME: 20 MINS** | **COOK TIME: 5–10 MINS** | **SKILL LEVEL: 1 (EASY)**

This is one of my favourite speedy weekday suppers. It only takes 10 minutes and requires almost no chopping, which I love! Zucchini noodles are the best pasta replacement as they have the exact same texture, but they're a little lighter and packed full of vitamins. They taste incredible tossed in this minty avocado and Brazil nut sauce with a heap of sautéed mushrooms on the top.

INGREDIENTS

For the noodles
4 zucchini
2 dozen (24) chestnut
    mushrooms
olive oil, for drizzling

For the avocado pesto
1 mug Brazil nuts
    (approx. 120 g)
4 avocados
4 tbsp olive oil
a large handful of fresh
    mint leaves
juice of 4 limes

DF, GF, V

METHOD

For the noodles: start by making the zucchini noodles, by simply putting the zucchini through your spiralizer. Alternatively, cut them into long matchsticks with a knife. Place the noodles to one side and begin the mushrooms.

Cut the mushrooms into thin slices, drizzle them with olive oil, and then gently heat them in a frying pan for about 5 minutes, until they're nice and soft.

For the avocado pesto: while the mushrooms cook, place the Brazil nuts in a food processor and blend for a minute or two, until they're totally crushed. Then add in the avocado flesh, olive oil, mint leaves, lime juice and a sprinkling of salt and pepper, and blend again.

Either mix the noodles and sauce together in a bowl raw and then add the mushrooms, or add the sauce and noodles to the mushrooms in the frying pan and gently heat for a couple of minutes to warm the dish up and soften the noodles a little.

SIMON WRIGHT
THE FRENCH CAFÉ

It's hard to beat a classic lemon meringue pie…
Zesty tangy lemon topped with clouds of sticky
meringue. There's an explosion of flavour and
texture in every mouthful. Bon appétit!

Simon

*Eden Terrace,
Auckland*

LEMON MERINGUE PIE

Recipe by *SIMON WRIGHT*, The French Café, Auckland, New Zealand

SERVINGS: 4–6 | **PREP TIME: 35 MINS PLUS RESTING** | **PREP TIME: 32 MINS** | **SKILL LEVEL: 3 (MORE CHALLENGING)**

INGREDIENTS

Pastry
225 g plain flour
pinch of salt
60 g caster sugar
150 g cold butter,
  cut into small cubes
1 egg yolk
25 ml cold water
4 Digestive biscuits,
  crushed

Lemon filling
zest of 6 lemons
375 ml lemon juice
150 ml water
60 g cornflour
450 g caster sugar
9 egg yolks
75 g butter

Meringue
200 g sugar
100 ml water
4 egg whites
pinch of cream of tartar
30 ml lemon juice
1 lemon

V

METHOD

For the pastry: place the flour, salt and sugar in a food processor and pulse together to mix. Add the butter and pulse until fully incorporated and the mixture resembles fine breadcrumbs. Add the egg yolk and the water, process until the mixture starts to come together and then tip the dough onto a clean work surface and gently knead together. Flatten it slightly with the palm of your hand, wrap in plastic wrap and refrigerate for 1 hour.

Lightly butter and flour a 23 cm x 4 cm pie dish with a removable base. Remove the pastry from the fridge, unwrap it and allow it to soften at room temperature for 10 minutes. Place half of the crushed biscuits on a clean work surface, place the pastry on top of the biscuits and roll the pastry out to about 3 cm thick. Sprinkle with the remaining biscuit crumbs and gently press them into the pastry with your rolling pin.

Line your prepared pie tin with the pastry. Roll your rolling pin across the top of the tin to remove excess pastry, then use your thumb and forefinger to crimp around the top of the pie tin so the pastry comes up above the edge. This will allow for a little shrinkage during cooking. Place the prepared pie tin back in the fridge to rest for 30 minutes.

Pre-heat your oven to 180°C. Line the pie tin with baking paper and baking beans and cook for 20 minutes. Remove the paper and beans and return to the oven for another 12 minutes or until the pastry is golden. Remove from the oven and allow the pastry to cool.

For the lemon filling: place the lemon zest, lemon juice and water in a heavy-based saucepan and whisk in the cornflour until the mixture is smooth. Add the sugar and egg yolks and stir until fully incorporated. Place over a medium heat and stir continuously until the mixture is warm, then add the butter and continue to stir until the mixture starts to boil and has thickened. Remove from the heat, pour the lemon filling into your prepared pie case and allow to cool fully at room temperature.

For the meringue: combine the sugar and water in a small saucepan and bring to the boil, stirring continuously with a wooden spoon until the sugar has dissolved. Reduce the heat slightly and continue to cook the syrup without stirring until it reaches 115°C on a sugar thermometer.

Place the egg whites in the bowl of an electric mixer fitted with a whisk attachment, add the cream of tartar and start whisking the egg whites until they reach soft peaks. Once the sugar syrup reaches 120°C, remove from the heat and slowly pour onto the whisking egg whites. Add the lemon juice and continue to beat on a medium speed until the meringue has cooled and is thick and glossy.

Remove the outside ring from the pie tin and place the pie on a serving dish. Spoon the meringue on top of the lemon filling, shaping it so it looks dramatic with spikes and curls. Finely grate the zest of the lemon over the meringue and carefully brown the meringue using a blowtorch. If you don't have a blowtorch, you can remove the meringue from the pie ring and place it under a hot oven grill to brown – this will take a matter of seconds.

ALDO ZILLI
CHEF & TV PRESENTER

I'm a fish chef – I love cooking fish; I love eating fish.
I grew up with fish – I come from a fishing village;
my dad was a fisherman and I got paid in fish when
I worked for fishermen.

Aldo

Covent Garden,
London

Aldo Zilli
San Carlo
CICCHETTI
BAR|RISTORANTE|CAFFÈ|CICCHETTI

BAKED COD WITH OLIVE CRUST & LENTILS

Recipe by *ALDO ZILLI*, chef & TV presenter, London, England

SERVINGS: 4 | **PREP TIME: 15 MINS** | **COOK TIME: 40 MINS** | **SKILL LEVEL: 1 (EASY)**

INGREDIENTS

100 ml extra virgin olive oil
1 carrot, diced
1 celery stalk, diced
1 onion, diced
500 g Puy lentils
2 bay leaves
1½ litres vegetable stock
1 tbsp breadcrumbs
1 tsp fresh rosemary leaves
1 tsp fresh thyme leaves
100 g black olives
4 cod fillets
  (about 180 g each)

DF

METHOD

Heat half the oil in a large pan and add the diced vegetables. Cook until soft, about 3–4 minutes, stirring to ensure they don't stick. Add the lentils and bay leaves, stir a couple of times, then add the stock and cook gently until it has been absorbed by the lentils (about 30 minutes). Keep warm.

Pre-heat the oven to 180°C/160°C fan.

In a food processor, blend the remaining oil with the breadcrumbs, herbs and black olives until you have a smooth mix.

Place the cod in a roasting tray and divide the olive mixture between the fillets, pressing it down with your fingers over the top and making sure you have an even distribution of the mix. Bake in the oven for 7–8 minutes. Serve the fish on top of the lentils.

JOCK ZONFRILLO
ORANA

I'm from an Italian Scottish family... Our Italian family dinners were typically hands everywhere, yelling and shouting and sauce up the walls — our staff dinners are no different! We're at work 18 hours a day and a staff meal is a great opportunity once a day for everyone to 'chew the fat'.

Jock

Adelaide, South Australia

LAMB, BEETROOTS, POTATOES & PEAS WITH EUCALYPTUS OIL

Recipe by *JOCK ZONFRILLO*, Orana, South Australia, Australia

SERVINGS: 4 | PREP TIME: 45 MINS | COOK TIME: 1 HOUR (APPROX.) | SKILL LEVEL: 2 (MODERATE)

INGREDIENTS

2 x lamb knuckles
  (I use black-faced
  Suffolk lamb)

4 medium-sized beetroots

4 waxy, yellow-fleshed
  potatoes, about the
  same size and shape

50 ml grapeseed oil

100 g butter, diced

2 cloves garlic,
  peeled and halved

4 sprigs thyme

2 sprigs rosemary

500 g fresh peas

100 ml jus or basic
  stock-based sauce

For the eucalyptus oil

a handful Eucalyptus
  brunnea leaves, plus
  extra for smoking
  (if you have access
  to one of these trees,
  brilliant; if not, substitute
  with parsley)

150 ml grapeseed oil

GF

METHOD

Cut the lamb knuckles in half lengthways and clean off any extra sinew (you can ask your butcher to do this for you). They can be cooked two ways: sous vide in a vacuum-sealed bag at 52°C for 1 hour or slow-smoked at about 130°C for about 1 hour. If cooking sous vide, let the meat rest for around 10 minutes before finishing (see below). If smoking, I recommend a temperature-controlled electric smoker, and allow the meat to rest for 20 minutes before finishing.

Meanwhile, pre-heat the oven to 150°C and bake the whole beetroots until wrinkled and soft, around an hour or so. Do not wrap them in anything, just place them directly onto a baking tray and into the oven. Once cool enough to handle, peel them and set aside for later. Leave the oven on (or reheat it when you are ready to serve).

While the beetroots are in the oven, quarter the potatoes lengthways and peel (I use a small paring knife and carefully peel the skin off to give a banana-like shape to the peeled potato and then cut a small indent in the straight side so that the potato pieces are an even thickness the whole way around). Heat the oil in a heavy-based frying pan and test the temperature by throwing a piece of potato in – there should be an instant sizzle and the potato will start to colour quickly. Throw the rest of the potatoes in and roll around until coloured and not sticking. At this stage the butter needs to be thrown in, one small piece at a time. Reduce the heat slightly and allow the butter to foam around the potatoes – there should be enough to submerge them. Throw in the garlic and the thyme and rosemary sprigs. The potatoes will be nicely golden by now. Continue cooking until soft in the centre, being careful to control the heat at all times. Once cooked, leave in a warm spot, in the butter, until all the other ingredients are ready.

Pod the peas and blanch them for 2 minutes in boiling water, then refresh in ice water before straining and setting aside.

For the eucalyptus oil: throw the leaves and the oil in a blender and blend on high for 5 minutes. Pass oil through a coffee filter paper or paper towels and set aside. If you are making parsley oil, blanch parsley briefly in boiling water and squeeze to remove excess water. Allow to dry until it is dry to the touch, then continue with blending and straining as for eucalyptus oil.

Throw the beetroots back in the oven to warm through. Once the lamb has rested, finish off by sealing it on the barbecue, preferably over an open flame so that you can throw a few eucalyptus leaves underneath to smoke the lamb nicely. Once sealed, allow to rest for a few minutes before carving. Toss the peas in a little butter over a medium heat with salt and white pepper.

To serve, place the beetroots first, one on each plate. Drain the potatoes a little on paper towel and place next to the beetroot. Carve the lamb, season and place on the plate, and sprinkle the peas over the top. Drizzle the eucalyptus or parsley oil over the top, along with a spoonful of jus to finish.

ADRIANO ZUMBO
PATISSIER

The marble cake was my first attempt at impressing friends at school
by baking for them. I'd make it with packet mix and food colouring
I nicked from my parents' supermarket! It really is priceless, the feeling
you get from making someone happy by cooking for them.

Rozelle,
New South Wales

GONE MARBLES CAKE

Recipe by *ADRIANO ZUMBO*, patissier, New South Wales, Australia

SERVINGS: 8–10 | **PREP TIME: 1 HOUR PLUS COOLING** | **COOK TIME: 60–80 MINS** | **SKILL LEVEL: 2 (MODERATE)**

INGREDIENTS

For the marble cake batter

150 g unsalted butter,
  at room temperature

240 g caster sugar

180 g egg whites,
  at room temperature

310 g plain flour

5 g baking powder

75 g cornflour

120 g almond meal

100 g crème fraîche

150 g 35%-fat cream

juice and zest of 1 orange

juice and zest of 1 lemon

assorted food colourings

milk or dark chocolate
  to decorate

For the chocolate ganache

340 g dark couverture
  chocolate (70%
  cocoa solids)

400 g 35%-fat cream

140 g unsalted butter

40 g glucose

V

METHOD

Pre-heat oven to 160°C and grease a 23 cm cake tin.

For the marble cake: in an electric mixing bowl with beater attachment, beat butter and sugar until softened and slightly lightened. Slowly add in egg whites, then add in dry ingredients. Add in crème fraîche and cream, and mix to combine. Lastly add in juices and zests, and continue mixing for 30 seconds until well combined. Divide the mixture into six bowls, 230 grams in each, and colour each one a different colour, stirring the colour through with a spoon.

Add coloured cake batters to the pre-greased tin in a random mix to form a marble effect. Bake for 60–80 minutes or until the centre is cooked and stable. Remove from oven and leave to cool in the tin for 15 minutes before turning out onto a wire rack to cool completely.

For the ganache: place dark chocolate in a food processor and blitz to make small pieces. In a saucepan place the cream, butter and glucose and heat to 65°C. Pour over the chocolate in the food processor and blitz until smooth and glossy. Pour into a container and cover with plastic wrap touching the surface of the ganache. Place in an air-conditioned cabinet or a cool space to set at room temperature.

To assemble: use a serrated knife to trim the top off the marble cake (it will have formed a slight peak which has cracked open), to make an even-sized cake. Cut the cake horizontally through the middle and separate the halves. Using a scraper, place some of the ganache on the bottom layer – enough to give roughly an 8 mm layer – and spread evenly using a palette knife or spatula. Place the top cake layer on, and cover with more ganache using the palette knife or spatula. Make the entire cake as smooth and neat as you can, covering the whole cake with ganache, then set aside.

For the decoration: for the initiated, spread some tempered chocolate, milk or dark, onto a marble top or a cold tray and leave to 'just' set. Using a palette knife, gently cut through whilst pulling down to form chocolate curls. Arrange the curls to your liking on top of the cake and serve. If you don't know how to temper chocolate, you can make chocolate curls using a vegetable peeler and a block of good-quality store-bought chocolate. At a pinch, you can grate the chocolate as an alternative decoration.

CONVERSIONS CHARTS & INDEX

A WORLD OF DIFFERENCE

Everyone the world over grows, harvests and prepares food. But the way we measure, cook and even refer to food varies from country to country, region to region and even from city to town; and producers, chefs and cooks – anyone who prepares food – use varying references for the same thing. For example, what someone in England calls a kitchen counter is known in New Zealand as a kitchen bench – and locally as 'the bench'. See opposite for a list of words that vary between places.

Of course the different ways ingredients are measured can cause the most confusion. For ease, we have provided metric measurements in the recipes and have included imperial conversion charts on pages 346–47. In simple terms, the closest equivalent imperial measurement is given for each metric measurement: cups are metric, i.e. 250 ml (so cooks in the United States may need to adjust a little), and pints are 20 fl oz in the United Kingdom and 16 fl oz in the United States. When in doubt, use the tables to convert metric measurements. As a last note on measurements, the Australian tablespoon measure is an anomalous 20 ml rather than 15 ml. Be warned...

Eggs used in the recipes are mostly medium-size, around 50 g (check the chart below for your local equivalent). The fat content in cream also varies between countries, and a rough guide is included here as well.

In summary, whilst maths is important, it isn't everything; if you're not sure you've got your conversions right, add ingredients bit by bit and keep tasting until you're happy with the result.

If in doubt, taste!

EQUIVALENT WORDS

00 flour	Italian milled flour used for pasta making (also called Doppio Zero)
bain marie	double boiler
baking paper	parchment paper
baking tray	cookie sheet
barbecue, grill	broil, braai
biscuit	cookie
broad bean	fava bean
capsicum	pepper, bell pepper
caster sugar	superfine sugar
celeriac	celery root
chilli	chili pepper
chilly bin	cool-box
coriander (fresh)	cilantro
cornflour	cornstarch (in the United States, corn flour is finely ground cornmeal rather than the finely ground white starch extracted from maize kernels, which is known as cornstarch)
cornmeal	maize meal
cos lettuce	romaine lettuce
Demerara sugar	light-brown cane sugar
digestive biscuit	Graham cracker
eggplant	aubergine
filo pastry	phyllo pastry
flaky salt	salt flakes, kosher salt, Maldon salt
food processor	processor, electric mixer
French bean	string bean (see also runner bean)
frying pan	skillet
golden syrup	corn syrup (these products are derived from different sources but can be substituted for one another)
greaseproof paper	wax paper, waxed paper
icing	frosting
icing sugar	powdered sugar
jam	jelly
jelly, gelatine	jello
liquidiser	blender, Vitamix
minced beef	ground beef
molasses	treacle
oregano	origanum
paper towel	kitchen paper, absorbent paper
pasty	turnover, hand pie
plain flour	all-purpose flour, standard flour
plastic wrap	cling film, Saran wrap
rocket	arugula
runner bean	green bean
scone	biscuit
self-raising flour	self-rising flour
slow-cooker	crockpot
snowpeas	mange tout
sorbet	sherbet (sorbet is dairy free, whereas sherbet includes milk or fat)
spring onion	green onion, scallion
stovetop	hob, range
strong flour	bread flour, high-grade flour, hard flour
sultanas	golden raisins
swede	rutabaga, yellow turnip
sweetcorn	corn, maize
tinfoil	aluminium/aluminum foil
tomato paste	a thick, condensed purée available in tubes or cans (known in the UK as tomato purée)
tomato sauce	ketchup, catsup
work surface	bench, counter
zucchini	courgette

ABBREVIATIONS

g	gram
kg	kilogram
oz	ounce
lb	pound
mm	millimetre/millimeter
cm	centimetre/centimeter
in	inch
ml	millilitre/milliliter
fl oz	fluid ounce
tsp	teaspoon
dsp	dessertspoon
tbsp	tablespoon
°C	degrees Celsius
°F	degrees Fahrenheit

CUP & SPOON CONVERSIONS

The metric cup (1 cup = 250 ml) is used in most countries outside the United States.

spoon/cup	metric	US metric
½ tsp	2½ ml	2½ ml
1 tsp	5 ml	5 ml
1 dsp	10 ml	–
1 tbsp	15 ml	15 ml
1 tbsp (Australia)	20 ml	–
⅛ cup	30 ml	30 ml
¼ cup	65 ml	60 ml
⅓ cup	85 ml	80 ml
½ cup	125 ml	120 ml
⅔ cup	170 ml	160 ml
¾ cup	190 ml	180 ml
1 cup	250 ml	240 ml
1½ cups	375 ml	360 ml
2 cups	500 ml	480 ml
4 cups	1 litre	960 ml

EGG SIZES

Each country has different minimal legal weights; the following weights are approximated for the purposes of conversion.

	Australia	NZ	South Africa	UK	US
around 35 g	–	Pullet (4)	Small	–	Peewee
around 43 g	Medium	Small (5)	Medium	Small	Small
around 53 g	Large	Standard (6)	Large	Medium	Medium
around 60 g	Extra Large	Large (7)	Very Large	Large	Large
around 70 g	Jumbo	Jumbo (8)	Jumbo	Very Large	Extra Large
around 75 g	King Size	–	Super Jumbo	–	Jumbo

CREAM EQUIVALENTS

Fat contents differ widely, but approximate conversions are as below. New Zealand only has one main type of cream, so you may need to adjust recipes that call for double cream by for example, adding extra gelatine for a panna cotta, or simmering a cream sauce for longer. Both single and double cream are now widely available in most countries.

Australia	NZ	South Africa	UK	US
Light	Lite	Pouring	Single	Light
Single	Cream	Pouring	Single	Light
Thickened	Thickened	Whipping	Whipping	Light Whipping
Double	Cream	Double Thick	Double	Heavy

WEIGHT CONVERSIONS

metric	*imperial/US*
15 g	½ oz
30 g	1 oz (= 28 g, more precisely)
60 g	2 oz
90 g	3 oz
100 g	3½ oz
125 g	4½ oz
150 g	5 oz
175 g	6 oz
200 g	7 oz
225 g	8 oz
250 g	9 oz
300 g	10½ oz
325 g	11½ oz
350 g	12½ oz
375 g	13 oz
400 g	14 oz
450 g	16 oz (1 lb)
500 g	18 oz
1 kg	36 oz (2¼ lb)

Note: 1 stick butter = 4 oz (112 g)

LIQUID CONVERSIONS

metric	*imperial/US*
5 ml	⅙ fl oz
15 ml	½ fl oz
30 ml	1 fl oz (= 28 ml, more precisely)
60 ml	2 fl oz
90 ml	3 fl oz
100 ml	3½ fl oz
125 ml	4 fl oz (¼ pint US)
150 ml	5 fl oz (¼ pint imperial)
175 ml	6 fl oz
200 ml	7 fl oz
225 ml	8 fl oz (½ pint US)
250 ml	9 fl oz
280 ml	10 fl oz (½ pint imperial)
340 ml	12 fl oz (¾ pint US)
420 ml	15 fl oz (¾ pint imperial)
450 ml	16 fl oz (1 pint US)
500 ml	18 fl oz
560 ml	20 fl oz (1 pint imperial)
1 litre	36 fl oz (1¾ pints imperial, 2¼ pints US)

LENGTH CONVERSIONS

metric	*imperial/US*
½ cm (5 mm)	¼ in
1 cm	½ in
2.5 cm	1 in
5 cm	2 in
7½ cm	3 in
10 cm	4 in
12½ cm	5 in
15 cm	6 in
18 cm	7 in
20 cm	8 in
23 cm	9 in
25½ cm	10 in
28 cm	11 in
30 cm	12 in (1 foot)
40 cm	16 in

OVEN TEMPERATURES

	Celsius	*Fahrenheit*	*Gas*
very cool	110°C	225°F	¼
	120°C	250°F	½
cool	140°C	275°F	1
	150°C	300°F	2
moderate	170°C	325°F	3
	180°C	350°F	4
moderate–hot	190°C	375°F	5
	200°C	400°F	6
hot	220°C	425°F	7
	230°C	450°F	8
very hot	240°C	475°F	9
	260°C	500°F	10

INDEX

The Beetroot Harvest, remoulade 322, *323*

The Ivy's Moroccan Spiced Rump Of Lamb with Hummus, Harissa & Smoked Eggplant 176, *177*

Walnut Bagna Càuda 80, *81*

Zucchini Noodles with Avocado Pesto 324, *325*

DAIRY FREE

Ale-Battered King George Whiting with Hand-Cut Chips 114, *115*

Avocado, Poached Eggs, Sourdough, Fermented White Cabbage & Fennel with Some Stuff From the Garden, aka Avocado Toast 276, *277*

Baked Cod with Olive Crust & Lentils 332, *333*

Berry Coulis 156, *157*

Berry Jam 156, *157*

Biltong 210, *211*

Bone Broth 210, *211*

Burnt Garlic, Chilli & Lemon Squid 146, *147*

Cashew & Macadamia Milk 204, *205*

Cha Giò, Vietnamese Spring Rolls 138, *139*

Chia Seed Chai Butternut Breakfast Pudding 122, *123*

Chickpea Kebabs *290–1,* 293

Confit De Canard, Preserved Duck Legs 200, *201*

Coq au Vin, Chicken Braised in Red Wine 130, *131*

Farro with Roasted Leeks & Smoky-Sweet Romesco 152, *153*

Meatloaf with Italian Flavours 222, *223*

Octopus a la Parrilla & Runner Bean Salad, Barbecued Octopus Salad 310, *311*

Oka I'a, Raw Fish & Coconut Salad 216, *217*

Oysters with Finger Lime, Carrot Foam & Avocado Cream 64, *65*

Pan-Fried Barramundi with a Salad Of Raw Zucchini & Fresh Herbs 228, *229*

Pommes Sarladaises, Potatoes in Duck Fat 200, *201*

Rabbit Casserole with Brandy & Prunes 76, *77*

Raspberry Milkshake (Hold the Milk) 204, *205*

Rick Stein's Shrimp & Dill Fritters with Ouzo 298, *299*

Salt & Pepper Squid with Lemon & Garlic Mayo 114, *115*

Shaved Raw Brussels Sprout Salad with Hazelnuts, Pomegranate & Pumpkin Seeds 260, *261*

Shaved Vegetables 134, *135*

Simplest Beef Stew 20, *21*

Spicy Prawn Tortillas 264, *265*

Spicy Vietnamese Chicken Wings 172, *173*

Sticky Meat Soup, Hearty Braised Lamb Shanks 252, *253*

Stir-Fried Hokkien Noodles with Chicken, Chilli & Bean Sprouts 160, *161*

Summer Roast Chicken 144, *145*

Syrian Fattoush Salad 168, *169*

Tamarind Prawns & Eggplant 186, *187*

The Beetroot Harvest 322, *323*

The Ivy's Moroccan Spiced Rump Of Lamb with Hummus, Harissa & Smoked Eggplant 176, *177*

Three Dhal Curry 12, *13*

Tortilla De Patatas, Spanish Omelette 50, *51*

Umleqwa, Farm Chicken 236, *237*

Wood-Roasted Reef Fish with Pineapple Curry 126, *127*

DESSERTS

Apple & Berry Crumble with Vanilla Custard 68, *69*

Apricot & Almond Torte 28, *29*

Bakewell Pudding 22, *23*

Banana Tarte Tatin with Rum & Raisin Ice Cream 150, *151*

Cherry Clafoutis 30, *31*

Chia Seed Chai Butternut Breakfast Pudding 122, *123*

Chocolate, Quince & Almond Tart 26, *27*

Lemon Meringue Pie 328, *329*

Normandy Tart Made with a Food Processor 178, *179*

Risogalo, George's Rice Pudding 48, *49*

Roasted Plums with Cardamom Caramel 16, *17*

Tarte Fine au Citron, Lemon Tart 286, *287*

ENTRÉES

'Nduja Bruschetta 294, *295*

Biltong 210, *211*

Cha Giò, Vietnamese Spring Rolls 138, *139*

Deep-Fried Stuffed Olives 54, *55*

Mezze Platter Favourites 194, *195*

Oysters with Finger Lime, Carrot Foam & Avocado Cream 64, *65*

Spanakopita Spirals 282, *283*

Walnut Bagna Càuda 80, *81*

Zucchini Soup with Chard Bruschetta 312, *313*

GLUTEN FREE

Abruzzo-Style Pork Stew with Roasted Capsicum, Chilli & Fennel 120, *121*

Agria Potato & Celeriac Gratin 76, *77*

Beetroot & Snapper Lasagne 134, *135*

Beetroot Raita *290–1,* 292

Berry Coulis 156, *157*

Berry Jam 156, *157*

Biltong 210, *211*

Bone Broth 210, *211*

Braai Freedom-Fighter Burger 34, *35*

Braaied Zucchini with Tortillas & Pesto 90, *91*

Bruce Gordon's Soufflé Omelette 110, *111*

Burnt Garlic, Chilli & Lemon Squid 146, *147*

Burrata with Lentils & Basil Oil 240, *241*

Butter Duck *290–1,* 292

Cashew & Macadamia Milk 204, *205*

Charmaine Solomon's Traditional Christmas Cake 296, *297*

Chia Seed Chai Butternut Breakfast Pudding 122, *123*

Chickpea Kebabs *290–1,* 293

Confit De Canard, Preserved Duck Legs 200, *201*

Fantastic Fish Pie 246, *247*

Fried Rice 182, *183*

John Dory with Curry Sauce, Cabbage & Shallots 256, *257*

Lamb, Beetroots, Potatoes & Peas with Eucalyptus Oil 336, *337*

Octopus a la Parrilla & Runner Bean Salad, Barbecued Octopus Salad 310, *311*

Oka I'a, Raw Fish & Coconut Salad 216, *217*

Oysters with Finger Lime, Carrot Foam & Avocado Cream 64, *65*

Pan-Fried Barramundi with a Salad Of Raw Zucchini & Fresh Herbs 228, *229*

Paneer Tikka *290–1,* 293

Papizza 232, *233*

Pommes Sarladaises, Potatoes in Duck Fat 200, *201*

Pork & Beans 272, *273*

Raspberry Milkshake (Hold the Milk) 204, *205*

Risotto con Piselli, Limone e Ricotta, Pea, Ricotta & Lemon Zest Risotto 280, *281*

Salad of Watermelon, Fennel, Peas & Feta 84, *85*

Salt & Pepper Squid with Lemon & Garlic Mayo 114, *115*

Shaved Raw Brussels Sprout Salad with Hazelnuts, Pomegranate & Pumpkin Seeds 260, *261*

Shaved Vegetables 134, *135*

Slaw with Pears, Toasted Hazelnuts & Buttermilk Dressing 116, *117*

Spicy Vietnamese Chicken Wings 172, *173*

Sticky Meat Soup, Hearty Braised Lamb Shanks 252, *253*

Summer Roast Chicken 144, *145*

Syrian Fattoush Salad 168, *169*

Tagliata Di Manzo, Thinly Sliced Rare Pan-Fried Beef with Balsamiac-dressed Salad 268, *269*

Tamarind Prawns & Eggplant 186, *187*

The Beetroot Harvest 322, *323*

The Ivy's Moroccan Spiced Rump Of Lamb with Hummus, Harissa & Smoked Eggplant 176, *177*

Three Dhal Curry 12, *13*

Tortilla De Patatas, Spanish Omelette 50, *51*

Wood-Roasted Reef Fish with Pineapple Curry 126, *127*

CONTRIBUTORS

Abrahams, Cass 10
Facebook: Cass Abrahams Cape Cuisine

Aikens, Tom 14
tomaikens.co.uk

Alexander, Stephanie AO 18
stephaniealexander.com.au

Baker, Gerard 22
Chef, food historian & radio presenter

Beer, Maggie AM 24
maggiebeer.com.au

Berry, Mary CBE 28
maryberry.co.uk

Blanc, Raymond OBE, CLH 30
raymondblanc.com

Braai, Jan 32
braai.com

Brettschneider, Dean 36
globalbaker.com

Brown, Al MNZM 38
albrown.co.nz

Brown, Jacob 42
thelarder.co.nz

Calombaris, George 46
georgecalombaris.com.au

Camorra, Frank 50
movida.com.au

Carluccio, Antonio OBE, OMRI 52
antonio-carluccio.com

Del Conte, Anna OMRI 56
Food writer

Donovan, Clayton 62
jaaningtree.com.au

Dunn, Rodney 66
theagrariankitchen.com

Du Toit, Erreida 70
huiskok.com

Emett, Josh 74
ratadining.co.nz

Erskine, Gizzi 78
Twitter: Gizzierskine

Fassnidge, Colin 82
fourinhand.com.au

Fehlmann, Skye 86
naturallyorganic.co.za

Flower, Tui 90
Cook & food writer

Fulton, Margaret OAM & **Suzanne Gibbs** 94
margaretfulton.com

Gault, Simon 100
simongault.com

Gilmore, Peter 104
quay.com.au

Gordon, Peter ONZM 108
peter-gordon.net

Govan, Nikki & Doug 112
starofgreece.com.au

Gyngell, Skye 116
springrestaurant.co.uk

Hafner, Brigitte 118
gertrudeenoteca.com

Hemsley, Melissa & Jasmine 122
hemsleyandhemsley.com

Holloway, Nick 124
nunu.com.au

Holst, Dame Alison DNZM CBE QSM 128
holst.co.nz

Holuigue, Diane OAM 130
The French Kitchen

Honeyman, Nick 132
parisbutter.co.nz
restaurant-le-petit-leon.fr

Hong, Angie & Dan 136
Twitter: Dan_Hong

Hoy Fong, Anthony 140
Twitter: Anthonyhoyfong

Hunter, Dan 142
braerestaurant.com

Hussain, Nadiya 146
Twitter: Begumnadiya

Johnson, Philip 148
eccobistro.com.au

Jones, Anna 152
annajones.co.uk

Julians Berry Farm 154
juliansberryfarm.co.nz

Kwong, Kylie 158
billykwong.com.au

Lawson, Nigella 162
nigella.com

Le Clerc, Julie 166
julieleclerc.com

Le, Minh 170
theforagingquail.com.au

Lee, Gary 174
the-ivy.co.uk

Leith, Prue OBE CBE 178
prue-leith.com

Liong, Victor & Evelyn 180
leehofook.com.au

Manfield, Christine 184
christinemanfield.com

Manfredi, Stefano 188
stefanomanfredi.com

Manifis, Peter 192
Incontro

Martin, James 196
jamesmartinchef.co.uk

For both the Nelson Mandela Foundation and for me, this book means we'll be able to touch and change lives with food; it's in everyone's hands to help make a difference.

Sello Hatang
Chief Executive, Nelson Mandela Foundation

The Nelson Mandela Foundation has partnered with Food & Trees for Africa in pursuit of its mission to develop and support community food and agricultural projects that will improve the lives of those who are in need of food and who need to be freed from poverty – a vision shared by both organisations.

The Nelson Mandela Foundation is a non-profit organisation focused on memory, dialogue and legacy work, founded by Nelson Mandela in 1999. They are the custodian of his life and times; they are a committed facilitator of his living legacy; and they are mandated to promote his lifelong vision of freedom and equality for all.

The Nelson Mandela Foundation delivers to the world an integrated, dynamic and trusted resource on the legacy of Nelson Mandela and, with this, its mandate to promote his vision and work by convening dialogues and creating platforms for engagement around critical issues to promote social justice.

Its vision, like that of its founder, Nelson Mandela, and the movement he spearheaded, is to contribute to the making of a just society that remembers its past, listens to all voices, and pursues social justice for all.

NELSON MANDELA
FOUNDATION
Living the legacy

nelsonmandela.org

Food & Trees for Africa is an organisation dedicated to advancing and promoting greening, climate-change action, sustainable natural resource management, permaculture food security and organic farming. To date they are responsible for the planting of over 4.2 million trees and thousands of permaculture food gardens, bamboo projects and organic farms in low-income communities across South Africa.

trees.co.za

359

ACKNOWLEDGEMENTS

We are grateful to everyone who contributed to the making of any of the 'great' cookbooks – *The Great Australian Cookbook*, *The Great New Zealand Cookbook*, *The Great South African Cookbook* and *The Really Quite Good British Cookbook* – and therefore enabled this book to be possible.

We would especially like to thank the respective editors: Helen Greenwood and Melissa Leong, who so eloquently persuaded all of the Australian contributors; Tim Harper, Wendy Nixon and Murray Thom, who literally and figuratively travelled the length and breadth of New Zealand; Libby Doyle, Jules Mercer and Ingeborg Pelser, who were a South African dream team; and food writer and editor extraordinaire William Sitwell and his indomitable British team, Tabitha Hawkins and Rosie Ramsden.

To the photographers and videographers who have travelled the world, your images and film have illuminated the books to the delight of readers and home cooks everywhere: Thank you to Lottie Hedley and Hayley Thom, whose intrepid pursuit of the ultimate shot in Australia and New Zealand knew no bounds; Toby Murphy and Brad Theron in South Africa, who so beautifully captured the essence of that stunning landscape; and Lizzie Mayson in Great Britain, who charmed everyone she came into contact with, including us. Thank you also to South African artist Conrad Botes for his original and iconic image of Nelson Mandela.

A very special thank you to Sello Hatang and the team at the Nelson Mandela Foundation: Lee Davies, Yase Godlo, Verne Harris, Heather Henriques, Molly Loate, Nkateko Mabale, Reabetwe Makwela, Palesa Manare, Limpho Monyamane, Neeran Naidoo, Lunga Nene, Mongezi Njaju and Buyi Sishuba. nelsonmandela.org

Huge thanks to the publishing team at PQ Blackwell: Rachel Clare, Liam Cooper, Helene Dehmer, Lisette du Plessis, Cameron Gibb, Ben Harris, Stefanie Lim and Kate Raven, and Paul and Liz Blackwell. We couldn't do any of it without you.

And finally, to all the chefs, cooks, bakers and food heroes who agreed to be part of this book – thank you. We're profoundly grateful for your generosity.

Ruth Hobday and Geoff Blackwell
PQ Blackwell

The publisher is grateful for literary permissions to reproduce items subject to copyright. Every effort has been made to trace the copyright holders and the publisher apologises for any unintentional omission. We would be pleased to hear from any not acknowledged here and undertake to make all reasonable efforts to include the appropriate acknowledgement in any subsequent editions.

Featured British recipes from the British publications listed below and the forthcoming THE REALLY QUITE GOOD BRITISH COOKBOOK, ed. William Sitwell, produced by PQ Blackwell Ltd, © PQ Blackwell Ltd pqblackwell.com.

Featured Australian recipes from the Australian publication listed opposite and THE GREAT AUSTRALIAN COOKBOOK, eds. Helen Greenwood and Melissa Leong, published by PQ Blackwell Ltd 2015, © PQ Blackwell Ltd pqblackwell.com/Thom Productions thomproductions.com.

Featured New Zealand recipes from the New Zealand publication listed below and THE GREAT NEW ZEALAND COOKBOOK created by Murray Thom and Tim Harper, published by PQ Blackwell Ltd 2014, © PQ Blackwell Ltd pqblackwell.com/Thom Productions thomproductions.com.

Featured South African recipes from THE GREAT SOUTH AFRICAN COOKBOOK, eds. Libby Doyle, Ruth Hobday, Jules Mercer and Ingeborg Pelser, published by Quivertree Publications in association with PQ Blackwell Ltd 2016, © PQ Blackwell Ltd pqblackwell.com/Quivertree Publications quivertreepublications.com.

TOM AIKENS
Roasted Plums with Cardamom Caramel adapted from *Easy* by Tom Aikens, published by Ebury Press. Text © Tom Aikens 2011. Reproduced by permission of The Random House Group Ltd.

GERARD BAKER
Bakewell Pudding adapted from *Mrs Beeton's Puddings* by Isabella Beeton and Gerard Baker, published by Weidenfeld & Nicolson, The Orion Publishing Group Ltd, a Hachette UK company, 2012, text © Weidenfeld & Nicolson, 2012.

MARY BERRY
Mary Berry's Apricot & Almond Torte adapted from *At Home* by Mary Berry and Lucy Young, published by BBC Books, an imprint of Ebury Publishing, a Random House Group Company, 2013, text © Mary Berry 2013. Reproduced by permission of The Random House Group Ltd.

RAYMOND BLANC
Cherry Clafouti adapted from *Kitchen Secrets* by Raymond Blanc, © Raymond Blanc, 2011, Bloomsbury Publishing Plc.

ANTONIO CARLUCCIO
Deep-fried Stuffed Olives adapted from *Antonio Carluccio: The Collection* by Antonio Carluccio, published by Quadrille Publishing Ltd, 2012.

ANNA DEL CONTE
Rotolo di Spinaci al Burro e Formaggio (Spinach and Pasta Roll with Melted Butter and Parmesan) from *Amaretto, Apple Cake and Artichokes: The Best of Anna Del Conte* by Anna Del Conte, published by Vintage, 2006, © Anna Del Conte 1989, 1991, 2006. Reproduced by permission of The Random House Group Ltd.

GIZZI ERSKINE
Walnut Bagna Cauda adapted from *Gizzi's Healthy Appetite: Food to Nourish the Body and Feed the Soul* by Gizzi Erskine, published by Mitchell Beazley, a division of Octopus Publishing Group Ltd, a Hachette UK Company, 2015, text © Gizzi Erskine 2015.

SKYE GYNGELL
Slaw with Pears, Toasted Hazelnuts and Buttermilk Dressing adapted from *Spring: The Cookbook* by Skye Gyngell, published by Quadrille Publishing Ltd, 2015.

JASMINE & MELISSA HEMSLEY
Chia Seed Chai Butternut Breakfast Pudding adapted from *The Art of Eating Well* by Jasmine and Melissa Hemsley, published by Ebury Press. Text © Jasmine and Melissa Hemsley 2014. Reproduced by permission of The Random House Group Ltd.

NADIYA HUSSAIN
Burnt Garlic, Chilli and Lemon Squid adapted from *Nadiya's Kitchen* by Nadiya Hussain, photographs by Holly Pickering, published by Michael Joseph, an imprint of Penguin Books, 2016.

ANNA JONES
Farro with Roasted leeks and Smoky-sweet Romesco adapted from *A Modern Way to Eat: Over 200 Satisfying, Everyday Vegetarian Recipes (That Will Make You Feel Amazing)* by Anna Jones, published by Fourth Estate, 2014.

NIGELLA LAWSON
Chocolate Guinness Cake adapted from *Feast: Food That Celebrates Life* by Nigella Lawson, published by Chatto & Windus, a Penguin Random House Company, 2004, © Nigella Lawson 2004. Reproduced by permission of The Random House Group Ltd.

PRUE LEITH
Normandy Tart Made with a Food Processor adapted from *Leith's Cookery Bible* by Prue Leith and Caroline Waldegrave, © Prue Leith and Caroline Waldegrave, 1991 and 2003, Bloomsbury Publishing Plc.

JAMES MARTIN
Sausage, Radicchio and Lemon Gnocchi adapted from *Home Comforts* by James Martin, published by Quadrille Publishing, 2014, text © James Martin 2014.

PIPPA MIDDLETON
Traditional Roast Rib of Beef from *Celebrate: A Year of British Festivities for Families and Friends* by Pippa Middleton, published by Michael Joseph, an imprint of Penguin Books, 2012.

RUSSELL NORMAN
Burrata with Lentils and Basil Oil adapted from *Polpo: A Venetian Cookbook (Of Sorts)* by Russell Norman, © Russell Norman 2012, Bloomsbury Publishing Plc.

JAMIE OLIVER
Fantastic Fish Pie adapted from *The Return of the Naked Chef* by Jamie Oliver, published by Michael Joseph, an imprint of Penguin Books, 2000, © Jamie Oliver Limited 2000.

YOTAM OTTOLENGHI
Pea and Mint Croquettes adapted from *Plenty More* by Yotam Ottolenghi, published by Ebury Press, 2014, text © Yotam Ottolenghi 2014. Reproduced by permission of The Random House Group Ltd

NATHAN OUTLAW
John Dory with Curry Sauce, Cabbage and Shallots adapted from *Nathan Outlaw's Fish Kitchen* by Nathan Outlaw, published by Quadrille Publishing Limited, 2014.

TOM PARKER BOWLES
Veal Holstein adapted from *Let's Eat* Meat by Tom Parker Bowles, published by Pavilion Books, an imprint of Avona Books Company Ltd, 2014, text © Tom Parker Bowles 2012.

LORRAINE PASCALE
Shaved Raw Brussels Sprout Salad with Hazelnuts, Pomegranate and Pumpkin Seeds adapted from *Eating Well Made Easy: Deliciously Healthy Recipes for Everyone, Every Day* by Lorraine Pascale, published by HarperCollins Publishers 2015, text © Lorraine Pascale.

FRANCES QUINN
Basic Flapjacks adapted from *Quinntessential Baking* by Frances Quinn, © Frances Quinn, 2015, Bloomsbury Publishing Plc.

THEO RANDALL
Tagliata di Manzo (Thinly Sliced Rare Pan-fried Beef with Balsamiac-dressed Salad) adapted from *My Simple Italian: 100 Inspired Recipes from One of Britain's Best Italian Chefs* by Theo Randall, published by Ebury Press, 2015. Reproduced by permission of The Random House Group Ltd

CLAUDIA RODEN
Almodrote de Berenjena (Eggplant Flan) adapted from *The Book of Jewish Food: An Odyssey from Samarkand to New York* by Claudia Roden, published by Penguin, 1996.

RUTH ROGERS
Pea, Ricotta and Lemon Zest Risotto adapted from *River Café Cookbook Green* by Rose Gray and Ruth Rogers, published by Ebury Press, 2000, text © Rose Gray and Ruth Rogers 2000. Reproduced by permission of The Random House Group Ltd.

MICHEL ROUX
Tarte Fine au Citron adapted from *Desserts* by Michel Roux, published by Quadrille Publishing Ltd, 2011.

NIGEL SLATER
'nduja Bruschetta adapted from *A Year of Good Eating: The Kitchen Diaries III* by Nigel Slater, published by Fourth Estate, 2015.

CHARMAINE SOLOMON
Charmaine Solomon's Traditional Christmas Cake adapted from *The Complete Asian Cookbook* by Charmaine Solomon, published by Hardie Grant Books, 2011, © Hardie Grant Books.

RICK STEIN
Shrimp and Dill Fritters with Ouzo adapted from *From Venice to Istanbul* by Rick Stein, published by BBC Books, 2015. Reproduced by permission of The Random House Group Ltd.

VALENTINE WARNER
Zucchini Soup adapted from *The Good Table: Adventures In and Around My Kitchen* by Valentine Warner, published by Mitchell Beazley, a division of Octopus Publishing Group Ltd, a Hachette UK Company, 2011, text © Valentine Warner 2011.

ELLA WOODWARD
Zucchini Noodles with Avocado Pesto adapted from *Deliciously Ella: Awesome Ingredients, Incredible Food That You and Your Body Will Love* by Ella Woodward, published by Yellow Kite, a Hodder & Stoughton, Hachette UK Company, 2015, © Ella Woodward 2015.

SIMON WRIGHT
Lemon Meringue Pie recipe by Simon Wright adapted from *The Great New Zealand Baking Book*, published by PQ Blackwell Ltd 2016, © PQ Blackwell Ltd pqblackwell.com/Thom Productions thomproductions.com.

ALDO ZILLI
Baked Cod with Olive Crust & Lentils adapted from *Zilli Light* by Aldo Zilli, published by Simon & Schuster Ltd, 2010.